The Gülen Movement

D1414278

Helen Rose Ebaugh

The Gülen Movement

A Sociological Analysis of a Civic
Movement Rooted in Moderate Islam

 Springer

Helen Rose Ebaugh
Department of Sociology
University of Houston
Houston, TX, USA
ebaugh@uh.edu

ISBN 978-1-4020-9893-2   e-ISBN 978-1-4020-9894-9
DOI 10.1007/978-1-4020-9894-9
Springer Dordrecht Heidelberg London New York

Library of Congress Control Number: 2009934510

© Springer Science+Business Media B.V. 2010
No part of this work may be reproduced, stored in a retrieval system, or transmitted in any form or by any means, electronic, mechanical, photocopying, microfilming, recording or otherwise, without written permission from the Publisher, with the exception of any material supplied specifically for the purpose of being entered and executed on a computer system, for exclusive use by the purchaser of the work.

Printed on acid-free paper

Springer is part of Springer Science+Business Media (www.springer.com)

Abstract

This is a book about Fethullah Gülen, a Turkish scholar and preacher, and the civic movement that he inspired in Turkey and ultimately throughout the world. During the decades of the 1960s, 1970s and 1980s, he preached to large crowds in mosques and public places throughout Turkey and wrote hundreds of newspaper columns, articles and books espousing his ideas. Gradually, many Turks from all walks of life responded to his ideas of education, modernization, positive relationships with the West and interfaith dialog by establishing dormitories, university preparatory courses and schools in which quality education, especially in the sciences and technology, were buttressed with commitment to Islamic ideals. With the fall of the Soviet Union, his ideas and service projects spread to the former Turkish-Soviet countries and ultimately to western Europe, North America, Asia, Africa, Australia and to Middle Eastern countries. Today, the Gülen-inspired movement has over 1,000 schools in 100 countries on 5 continents. It is a civic movement rooted in moderate Islam and committed to educating youth, fostering interfaith and intercultural dialog, assisting the needy in society and contributing to global peace. Based on interview data and visits to Gülen-inspired institutions in Turkey and in the United States, this book describes the movement with emphasis upon the structure and commitment mechanisms that both demonstrate commitment to the movement as well as simultaneously generating commitment on the part of movement participants.

Contents

Prologue

In May, 2005, I was invited to give the keynote address at the International Harran Conference in Göteborg, Sweden. All I knew was that it was to be an interfaith meeting of people from the Abrahamic religions, sponsored by the Swedish Ambassador to Turkey. After a quick Google search, I learned that Harran is a city in southeastern Turkey where the Prophet Abraham lived for a time and that this was the third Harran conference to focus on interfaith dialog. It was being held in Sweden this time so that the religious leaders from Turkey (e.g. the Armenian, Syrian and Greek Orthodox Patriarchs, several of the leading imams and Jewish rabbis) would be on neutral ground and not pressured by their respective constituencies. In the course of preparing my remarks, I had lunch with Lynn Mitchell, a professor of religion at our university, whom I knew had recently returned from an interfaith trip to Turkey, sponsored, he told me, by the local Gülen movement. The *what*, I asked him? He proceeded to describe Mr. Gülen, the religious scholar who was the inspiration behind the movement, as a moderate Muslim, devoted to furthering science and modernization through educational projects, and emphasizing globalization and interfaith dialog.

Professor Mitchell also invited me to a "Dialogue of Civilizations" seminar that he was co-sponsoring on campus devoted to exploring the ideas of Mr. Gülen. It was at the conference that I met two graduate students in the movement who were in our Department of Sociology and whose theses I later supervised. In my association with these and other students who followed them into our program, I learned more about the history, ideas, goals and service projects inspired by the movement. I was teaching courses in the Sociology of World Religions and, since 9/11, had been repeatedly asking where the moderate Muslim voice could be heard to counter the radical Islam that was continuously presented in the U.S. media. The more I learned about the Gülen movement, the more I thought that here was one example of moderate Islam that stood in opposition to much of what was being presented in the media.

During my first visit to Turkey in 2006 I visited a number of Gülen-inspired schools, including a university, and several hospitals that were built on ideals taught by Mr. Gülen. It was clear that this was a movement that was growing in Turkey as well as in the Turkish Diaspora around the world. It was also evident, from the quality of the institutions I visited, that this was a well-funded movement.

For decades my academic research focused on religious movements and, more recently, the impact of religious groups on the lives of the new immigrants settling in the United States and in Houston, Texas, in particular. I was becoming increasingly active within interfaith dialog circles. As a result, interest in the Gülen movement as a thriving transnational religious movement was a "natural" for me. In addition, I came to admire the many service projects sponsored by the movement, including the quality schools, top-notch hospitals, a thriving relief agency and the numerous interfaith events that were a hallmark of the movement.

From a sociological point of view, given the voluntary nature of movement participation and the non-hierarchical structure that was evident, I was especially interested in ways in which people were organized to maximize commitment to the goals and projects of the movement. A related issue involved the large amounts of money necessary to build and maintain the service projects. What was the source of the money? If, indeed, it came from individual contributions, what motivated people to donate?

To answer these questions I set about to conduct semi-structured interviews with a broad sample of people in Turkey and in Houston, Texas. The range and characteristics of people I interviewed is described in the "Introduction". Methodologically, my commitment was to be as objective and scientific as possible, posing questions, listening to responses and recording them as accurately as possible for analysis. Each person I interviewed knew that I was a university research professor attempting to understand the movement so that I could write a book describing the movement, its supporters and projects.

In addition to reporting what I heard, in the writing of this book I also brought to bear broader analytical interpretations embedded in my training as a sociologist. I was writing, therefore, not as an insider who understood the movement from within but rather as an academic outsider who listened to participants and tried to capture their perspectives as closely as possible while, simultaneously, bringing to bear an analytical perspective informed by my academic training. My goal while writing the book was to report as accurately as possible what I learned from those I interviewed while analyzing their remarks through the lens of sociological interpretation.

There are a number of people whom I would like to thank for their valuable contributions to this book. Dr. Y. Alp Aslandogan served as the translator for the interviews that I conducted in Turkey. In addition to his translation skills, I learned much about the history and culture of Turkey as we traveled between the Asian and European sides of Istanbul and around the cities in Turkey. At the outset of the project, Mr. Dogan Koc conducted interviews with businessmen in Ankara. Dr. Muhammed Cetin read the manuscript and made valuable suggestions, especially regarding historical and cultural facts that enhanced understanding of Mr. Gülen's contributions at the particular period in which he preached in Turkey. I talked with Professor Maria Curtis from the University of Houston, Clearlake, to get a better understanding of the role of women in the movement. Simay Ozlu-Diniz, a graduate student in our Sociology Department, assisted me with conducting the interviews with critics of the movement that I discuss in the

Appendix. My daughter, Sarah Ebaugh, read the manuscript and challenged me, especially in the final chapter, to be more explicit in my argument that the movement does not currently have the characteristics of a "dangerous" or sectarian movement. Willemijn Arts, my editor at Springer, was encouraging at every step in the publishing process and was delightful to work with. I thank each and every one of the people who spent their valuable time talking with me about the movement. This is really a book about them. And, finally, my husband, Albert L. Ebaugh, accompanied me on each of my four Turkey trips and to most of the interviews I conducted. He gets the prize for being an enthusiastic, supportive and involved partner.

Introduction

The terrorist attack on September 11, 2001, marked a watershed event not only for the United States but globally. Within hours of the events in New York and Washington, Muslims were targeted as the perpetrators. Suddenly, Americans riveted to their television and computer screens learned that Muslims were not only some amorphous group in the Middle East but lived in American neighborhoods, worked in American workplaces, and went to school in American universities and even with their children in grammar and high schools. People all over America were asking: Who are these people? What do they believe? How can a religion promote the destruction of thousands of human lives? Suddenly, the news media as well as people all over the United States were fixated on a religion that was foreign to most of them.

The following day, September 12, President Bush, while announcing his "war on terror," warned the American people that not all Muslims are terrorists and that Islam is a peaceful religion which does not condone violence. He took the lead in framing the previous day's events as the actions of a radical, extremist group within an otherwise peaceful religion. He called on Americans not to retaliate by attacking Muslims in their cities and neighborhoods.

Since 9/11 there has been a groundswell of interest in Islam in the United States, as evidenced by the increased number of books, newspaper stories, and magazine articles focused on Islam, the many television programs aimed at describing the beliefs and practices of Islam, and the mushrooming of a number of courses in universities on Islam and world religions in general. As a result, more Americans are learning about the many different forms of Islam, the fact that there are extremists in every religion, and that an entire religion cannot be blamed for the actions of a minority of members. However, there remains widespread misconceptions regarding Islam and there continues to be a tendency for many to equate Muslim and terrorist.[1]

---

[1] For survey data on attitudes of Americans regarding Muslims see Wuthnow (2005); Eck (2001); CAIR (2006).

H.R. Ebaugh, *The Gülen Movement: A Sociological Analysis of a Civic Movement Rooted in Moderate Islam*, DOI 10.1007/978-1-4020-9894-9_1,
© Springer Science+Business Media B.V. 2010

"Moderate" Islam

One response to Islamic radicalism on the part of Muslims worldwide has been the growth and visibility of "moderate" or nonviolent Muslim movements. One such movement that is experiencing rapid growth in Turkey, its country of origin, and also in the former countries of the Soviet Union, Europe, Australia, Canada, Africa and recently in the United States is the Gülen Movement. This movement is inspired by an Islamic scholar and former imam, Mr. Fethullah Gülen, who was born in Turkey in 1941, became an imam and famous preacher, teacher, author and poet in the 1970s and 1980s, and moved to the United States in 1999, where he currently lives. On the day after the 9/11 attacks, Mr. Gülen ran a full page statement in the *New York Times* in which he condemned the attacks and stated that the perpetrators were not representative of Islam. His message is one of tolerance, respect, interfaith dialog and centers on the need to create bridges between the Muslim world and the West. Mr. Gülen insists on the necessity of creating scientific and technological advances in the Muslim world achieved by means of education. As Ibrahim M. Abu-Rabi describes, "Gülen defends a 'progressive' notion of Islam in which Muslims are able to totally engage the world without any fear or prejudice."[2]

Even though many policy makers advocate the support of moderate Islam as a strategy for confronting Islamic radical groups, the term "moderate Muslim" is highly contested among scholars and policy makers[3] and among Muslims themselves, who argue that the term is used pejoratively to indicate a Muslim who is more secular and less Islamic than "the norm," which varies across communities.[4] Steven Cook, the Douglas Fellow at the Council on Foreign Relations, argues that moderation is in "the eye of the beholder" and that policymakers should focus on identifying those who can contribute pragmatic solutions to the problems in the region, "moderate" or not.[5] In the same vein, Jay Tolson contends that definitions of moderation reflect the ideological and political commitments of the definers, such that conservatives hold stricter, narrower views of moderation while liberals see more shades of acceptability.[6] While the term is thus contentious, I use it in the title of this book to indicate an Islamic group that is willing to co-exist peacefully with peoples of other faiths, supports democracy, cherishes freedom of thought and educational pursuits while recognizing the role of faith and religion, and condemns the use of violence in the name of Islam. Within these parameters, the Gülen Movement is one strong example of moderate Islam in the contemporary world.

---

[2] Abu-Rabi (2008).

[3] See Cook (2007) for a discussion of debates regarding the term "moderate Muslim."

[4] Mr. Gülen, himself, rejects the notion that his discourse represents a kind of "moderate Islam" since he argues that Islam is already moderate.

[5] Cook (2007).

[6] Tolson (2008).

Recent Media Attention to the Gülen Movement

Recently, a number of widely read and reputable journals have taken note of Mr. Gülen and the many service projects, such as schools, hospitals, dormitories and nonprofit charities that are inspired by the ideas that he is putting forth in his sermons, books, articles, CDs, web addresses, and personal visits with followers who come to his Pennsylvania home to spend time in his company and seek his advice. Forbes' *Oxford Analytica* published an article (01/18/2008) entitled "Gülen Inspires Muslims Worldwide" in which mention is made of the movement's "ability to mobilize considerable resources and for its influence among decision-makers." In May (05/04/2008) the *New York Times* printed a front page article on Gülen schools in Pakistan that offer "a gentler Islam" by providing a vision of Islam that is "moderate and flexible, comfortably coexisting with the West while remaining distinct from it." The French magazine, *Le Monde,* carried a story (11/05/2006) on the achievements of schools opened by Gülen followers in Germany, noting that these schools addressed the education problems of migrant children and could be taken as an example by German schools.

The *International Herald Tribune* (01/18/2008) wrote that Mr. Gülen was "an inspiration for Muslims who feel at home in the modern world." The article was also quoted by *Forbes* magazine. The *Economist* has recently published three articles on the movement. An article (01/30/2008) on the Kurdish problem in Turkey identifies Mr. Gülen as a "liberal Muslim cleric who lives in self-imposed exile in America." It also mentions that followers of Mr. Gülen distributed meat to some 60,000 families during the Feast of the Sacrifice and that doctors who are followers of Mr. Gülen are offering free check-ups and treatment in Kurdish regions, presenting the message that Kurds and Turks are brothers in Islam. A subsequent issue of the *Economist* (03/06/2008) carried two articles about the Gülen movement and praised the educational and service projects that it is providing worldwide. In addition, at the 2008 World Economic Forum Annual Meeting in Davos, Switzerland, a report entitled "Islam and the West: Annual Report on the State of Dialog" highlighted the Gülen movement's network of 100 schools scattered throughout central Asian countries as an example of a significant attempt to further dialog among cultures.

In August, 2008, *Foreign Policy* magazine asked readers to vote for the world's top public intellectual. Fethullah Gülen won in a landslide, probably due to millions of votes cast by his supporters who read about the poll in *Zaman,* a Turkish newspaper read by many people in the movement. Interestingly, the top ten intellectuals on the list are all Muslim, probably the result of votes cast by Gülen supporters who voted not only for their leader but for other Muslims in the poll. While the poll was not scientific in terms of random sampling of respondents, its results demonstrate the millions of Gülen supporters and the power of the network that unites them.

Since 2005, hundreds of Americans have become acquainted with the Gülen movement as a result of participating in interfaith trips to Turkey sponsored by local Gülen groups as well as Gülen hosts in Turkey. These dialog trips originated in Houston, Texas, and are now spreading throughout the United States. On these 8–10 day trips, participants are introduced to the major historical, cultural and religious sites in Turkey as well as provided the opportunity to interact with local Muslim families, many of whom are members of the Gülen movement. The purpose of these trips is, in no way, a recruiting device for the movement; rather, they are structured to promote interfaith dialog among religious groups in the U.S. and in Turkey. However, since the trips are lead by Gülen supporters, they usually include several dinners in the homes of Turkish Muslims who are part of the Gülen Movement and visits to several schools and hospitals supported by the movement, so people on these trips become familiar with it.

Given that the Gülen movement is grassroots-based and has no centralized bureaucracy, it is impossible to determine precisely how many people are involved, either as members or participants. However, estimates are that 10–15% of the 70 million people in Turkey are associated with the movement and 8 to 10 million members worldwide, located in over 100 countries on five continents.[7] Likewise, it is impossible to count the many and varied service projects that have been inspired by the ideas of Mr. Gülen and initiated by members in the movement. However, the best estimates are: over 1,000 schools located on five continents in the 100 countries where members reside; six top-notch private hospitals; one private university; hundreds of student dormitories and preparatory courses for the national university exam in Turkey; an international relief organization; local organizations of movement members throughout the world who sponsor interfaith dialog trips to Turkey, Iftar dinners to break the fast during Ramadan, and Gülen conferences and interfaith dialog events in regional and local areas.

Mr. Gülen and the Gülen Movement as a Lightning Rod

At the same time that the movement is thriving both in Turkey and worldwide, and perhaps because of its success, critics of Mr. Gülen and his movement have arisen who are vehemently opposed to the movement and who are afraid of its consequences for Turkey.[8] They fear that Mr. Gülen is attempting a political takeover of Turkey like that orchestrated by the Ayatollah Khomeini in the 1970s in Iran, a regime-change that overthrew the modernization efforts of the Shah and put in

---

[7] Agai (2003) estimates the Gülen followers run approximately 150 private schools, 150 educational centers, and an even larger number of dormitories in Turkey and over 250 educational institutions in nearly all parts of the world. Michel (2003) estimates that there are over 300 educational institutions (elementary and high schools, college preparatory institutions, dormitories and universities) in fifty different countries. Baskan's (2004) estimates are significantly higher: 2,000 schools in 52 countries on five continents, including 125 in Turkey; Kalyoncu (2008) states that there are over 500 educational and cultural institutions in over 90 countries.

[8] Yavuz (2003) discusses four areas in which Gülen and his movement are open to criticism in Turkey: (1) gender relations; (2) silence on the Kurdish question; (3) support for the 28 February 1997 soft coup; and (4) a duty-oriented, noncritical educational system.

place a very conservative, Islamist government. Likewise, critics fear that the movement will take Turkey backwards in terms of traditionalism, thus putting a halt to Turkey's modernization and attempts to be accepted into the European Union. Underlying these fears is the critics' contention that the West, especially the United States, is financing the service projects in the movement such as schools, hospitals, and its extensive media empire in order to establish a moderate Islamic presence in the Middle East as an antidote to radical Islamic terrorism. In summary, Mr. Gülen has become a lightning rod, creating a maelstrom not only in Turkey but throughout the entire world where his followers have migrated.

In November, 2007, the U.S. Citizenship and Immigration Service (USCIS) denied a U.S. Permanent Resident Card, commonly known as the "green card," to Mr. Gülen who had been living in the United States for nine years. He also lost the appeal he filed for reconsideration of the verdict. The court found the arguments that Mr. Gülen was an "extraordinarily talented academic" to be insufficient to merit permanent status as a scholar in the U.S. In the prosecutor's arguments, Gülen's financial resources were detailed, claiming that Saudi Arabia, Iran, the Turkish government and the CIA are financing the Gülen movement, which the U.S. State Department's attorneys estimated involved over $25 billion. On July 16, 2008, a federal court overturned the original decision based on lack of sufficient evidence and ordered the Secretary of Homeland Security to approve Mr. Gülen's original petition for a green card.[9] In October, 2008, the card was officially awarded to him by the United States government.

Eight years earlier, on August 31, 2000, Mr. Gülen was charged by the Turkish state prosecutor, Nuh Mete Yuksel, for organizing a movement to change the secular government established by Mustafa Kemal Ataturk in 1923 when Turkey became a republic and to turn it into a theocratic state. After years of court hearings and numerous investigations and court documents, on May 5, 2006, the case against Mr. Gülen was dismissed by the state security court and he was exonerated of any wrongdoing.[10]

Who is this man who has garnered such attention from the media, the judicial system and both his followers and his critics? Is he a Gandhi,[11] as some followers

---

[9] For a review of the case see http://arama.hurriyet.com for July 19, 2008; also: http://www.todayszaman.com for July 23, 2008.

[10] For discussion of this case see: Aslandogan (2006); also www.sundayszaman.com for October 21, 2007.

[11] Mohandas Karamchand Gandhi (1869–1948) was a major spiritual and political leader in India and a major figure behind the Indian independence movement. As a committed Hindu, he advocated non-violence, lived modestly in a self-sufficient residential community, ate simple vegetarian food and underwent long fasts as a means of self-purification and social protest. He led nationwide campaigns for eradicating poverty, expanding women's rights, building religious and ethnic harmony, ending untouchability, increasing economic self-reliance and advocating India's independence from foreign domination. He inspired civil rights and freedom movements across the world.

claim, or a Khomeini,[12] as many critics fear? Is he to be idolized and emulated or scorned and condemned as a tyrant? What is the Gülen movement that now claims millions of followers worldwide and is attracting such financial resources that suspicions are being raised that some government must be behind the movement? Where is the money coming from to build and sustain the hundreds of schools in over 100 countries, six top rated private hospitals, the largest newspaper in terms of readership in Turkey, the biggest Islamic bank in Turkey, and a relief organization that raises over $16 million annually to assist with disaster relief? Why is one Turkish man, almost 70 years old and in poor health, who now lives in the United States, the lightning rod of such vitriolic hatred and fear on the part of some Turkish citizens? What has made the Gülen movement so successful over the thirty or so years of its existence and what accounts for the fact that it is now expanding beyond Turkey to capture the involvement of both Turkish and non-Turkish people around the world?

The purpose of this book is to introduce Fethullah Gülen and the movement which he inspires to English-speaking readers and to answer the above questions with data gathered during field trips to Turkey and interviews with Gülen followers in Houston, Texas. Based on my conversations with colleagues around the country as well as audiences to whom I lecture and students in my classes at the University of Houston, it appears that Mr. Gülen and the Gülen Movement are unfamiliar to most Americans. However, as increasing media attention focuses on this movement and more and more Americans are participating in interfaith trips to Turkey and events sponsored by Gülen supporters in the United States, there is increasing interest in this thriving, moderate Turko-Islamic movement.

Theoretical Frameworks

There are two theoretical frameworks that help to explain why the Gülen movement has been so successful both in Turkey and internationally. The first, resource mobilization theory, sheds light on the human and financial resources that enable a movement to grow and succeed in its goals. The second, organizational commitment theory, focuses on movement strategies for garnering member motivation to provide necessary resources and the consequences of such commitment on building loyalty to the movement, thus assuring its vitality and growth.

---

[12] Ayatollah Ruhollah Khomeini (1900–1989) became an important Islamic scholar and leader in the Shiite religious resistance against the modernization of Iran during the 1960s. The Shah of Iran exiled him first to Turkey and then to Iraq where his influence grew. In response to his growing power, Saddam Hussein exiled him to Paris in 1978 where he continued to spread his conservative religious message, including his hatred of the West and his call for Islamic revolution. In 1978 Khomeini returned to Iran where his followers overthrew the Shah of Iran and installed Khomeini as leader of the country, a position that he held until 1989 when he died from cancer.

Resource Mobilization Theory

Resource mobilization is a sociological theory that emphasizes the types of resources that are necessary for the maintenance and growth of social movements. Earlier theory focused on the social psychology of movement participants, who were seen as people who are disgruntled with one or more aspects of society.[13] Resource mobilization theory, which emerged in the 1970s, views social movements as networks of people who are able to attract the types and amounts of finances and human labor to effect change in society.[14] According to resource mobilization theorists, there is always enough discontent in any society to provide grass-roots support for a movement. To focus and organize the discontent into a social movement, it is necessary for a core group of sophisticated strategists to organize to harness those disaffected people, to attract money and supporters, and to capture the media's attention, forging alliances with those in power and creating an organizational structure.[15] This theory assumes that without such resources, social movements cannot be effective and that dissent and disaffection alone are not sufficient to create social change via a social movement. If human and financial resources are not available to support the goals of the movement, it will eventually collapse or merge with a movement that is more successful in attaining resources. Resource mobilization theory, therefore, deals specifically with the dynamics and tactics of social movement growth, decline, and change.

Most resource mobilization theorists[16] agree that the following resources are necessary for a successful social movement: money, legitimacy, and labor. Sufficient and consistent streams of money make possible the salaries and support of movement staff; provide office space, computers, copying machines, etc that are essential to make visible and advertize the message and goals of the movement; publish ads, announcements, billboards, websites and other media venues to mobilize potential participants; and finance projects and events sponsored by the movement. Resource mobilization theory will be used, especially in Chapter 4, "the Network of Local Circles," and Chapter 6, "The Water for The Mill: Financing of Gülen-Inspired Service Projects", to frame and analyze the mechanisms whereby resources are garnered for the growth and success of the movement.

---

[13] Theorists who propose a social psychology perspective include Gurr (1970); Turner and Killian (1972); Smelser (1962); Byrne (1997); Eyerman and Jamison (1991).

[14] Oberschall (1973); Tilly (1978); Snow et al. (1980); McAdam et al. (1996); Melucci (1999); Edwards and McCarthy (2004).

[15] McCarthy and Zald (1977); Kendall (2005); Gamson and Fireman (1979).

[16] McCarthy and Zald (1977); Jenkins (1983); Edwards and McCarthy (2004); Garner (1996); McCarthy and Wolfson (1996).

Organizational Commitment Theory

Related to the issue of obtaining the resources needed for movement success is the question of motivation for membership involvement. Why are millions of people committed to the movement in terms of giving time, labor, emotional involvement and finances to achieve movement goals? Commitment involves identifying one's personal fate with the success or failure of the collectivity.[17] It is typically examined in terms of the mix of the personal and organizational characteristics which increase willingness to exert high levels of effort, to remain a member in the organization, to accept its major goals and values, and to value the organization as worthwhile.

Research by the sociologist, Rosabeth Kanter, in the late 1960s and early 1970s on commitment within U.S. communes[18] remains a classic statement on organizational mechanisms that generate member commitment. She was interested in how groups maintain cohesion and she focused on the organizational requirements that influence individuals to feel that their own self-interest is indistinguishable from that of the group – their sense of commitment. She argued that a person is committed to a relationship or group to the extent that he/she sees it as expressing or fulfilling some fundamental part of himself and identifies group goals as nourishing his/her own sense of self. A committed person is loyal and involved, has a sense of belonging, a feeling that the group is an extension of himself or herself and that he/she is an extension of the group.

In summary, resource mobilization and commitment theory provide a lens through which to view the Gülen Movement and to explain why it is thriving. These theoretical tools, along with an analysis of the historical and political context in which Fethullah Gülen preached in Turkey and an understanding of the Turkish/Islamic concepts of giving and hospitality, provide insight into the beliefs, values, and social dynamics that are propelling this movement to national and international prominence.

Research Questions

Based on resource mobilization and organizational commitment theory described above, there are three basic questions that guide the research reported in this book:

1. From a sociological perspective, what are the organizational commitment mechanisms that explain why the Gülen movement has captured the enthusiasm of millions of Turks within the country as well as in the countries to which they have migrated?

---

[17] Kanter (1972).
[18] Ibid.

2. In what ways do the financial mechanisms involved in funding the service projects promote the involvement, enthusiasm and commitment of movement supporters? How are supporters motivated to donate?
3. What are the financial arrangements related to the institutions that are associated with the Gülen movement and in what ways are supporters related financially to Gülen-inspired projects?

The research design that generated the data reported in this book result from the above research questions. I decided to visit Gülen-inspired institutions and to interview both administrators and staff within these organizations. In addition, I interviewed a wide array of people who support the movement, both financially and through their volunteer work. Since the motivation for service begins within the local circles that characterize the movement, I focused especially upon these groups.

It is as important to emphasize what the research design does **NOT** include as it is to delineate what is included. This is especially the case, given the highly ideologically charged topic that is the focus of this book. There are many critics of the movement both within Turkey and within the Turkish diaspora. While I did talk with some of these critics, I did not conduct systematic interviews based on a random or representative sample of interviewees. Since the critical perspective was not part of my original research design, this book is **not** an evaluation of the movement from various perspectives. Moreover, I do not present a critical evaluation of the historical or political role of the Gülen movement in Turkish society. Rather, my data are circumscribed by the three research questions raised above, all three of which are answered in terms of my interviews with supporters within the movement.

This book is a sociological analysis of the Gülen movement, based on my academic training as a sociologist. While Chapter 2, "Islam and the State Throughout Turkish History" does present a very brief history of the relation of Islam and the state throughout Turkish history, it is not intended as a scholarly historical work on the topic. Rather, I wrote that chapter in very broad terms to introduce the Western reader to the big contours of Turkish history that provide a context for the evolution of the Gülen movement, with emphasis upon relations between religion and state in Turkey. Likewise, Chapter 5 on "The Turkish–Islamic Culture of Giving" is offered in broad terms to acquaint the Western reader with historical and religious concepts that provide background for the service projects sponsored by the Gülen movement and to demonstrate that Mr. Gülen calls forth these cultural traits in motivating his supporters to initiate and be involved in serving the needy.

Sources of Data in the Book

Within the past three years, I have spent eight weeks in Turkey during four different visits, each lasting two weeks. These visits provided opportunity to experience both the culture of the country and the subculture of the Gülen movement.

During these visits I was able to visit approximately eight Gülen schools in Istanbul, Antalya, Izmir, Bursa, Ankara, Konya, and Urfa. I also interviewed doctors and administrators in four Gülen-inspired hospitals in these cities as well as visited businesses associated with the movement such as the Journalists and Writers Foundation, Samanyolu T.V. station, *Zaman* newspaper and Kimse Yok Mu, a relief organization. The first two visits were part of an interfaith dialog trip which I made along with about a dozen other people from the United States. We were hosted for meals and dialog in approximately ten homes by Turkish Muslims associated with the movement. These first two trips provided context and general familiarity with movement organizations and people in the movement in anticipation of my third visit, which was explicitly research oriented and interview focused.

In April, 2008, I spent two weeks in Istanbul, Bursa, and Mudanya conducting formal interviews with top administrators in Gülen-related institutions with the goal of documenting the financial history and structure of the organizations. I focused on how the organization or service project was initiated, costs associated with the original project, sources of financing, the history of financially sustaining the project over time and its current financial status, including expenses and sources of income. I was especially inquisitive regarding any government support for projects, including not only money but land, buildings, and tax breaks. The Gülen-related institutions and projects included in my interviews are:

- Bank Asya
- Samanyolu television station
- *Zaman* newspaper
- The Journalists and Writers Foundation
- Fatih University
- Hospitals: Sema Hospital, Istanbul; Bakar Hospital, Bursa
- Three Gülen-inspired schools
- Kimse Yok Mu Relief Organization

Each interview was recorded with permission of the people involved and then later transcribed for easier analysis.

In addition, I conducted interviews with a cross section of people who are participants in the Gülen movement. Some of these interviews were one on one with individuals who contribute time and money to service projects; others were focus groups with various local circles of Gülen members. I interviewed two groups of businessmen who are major supporters of movement projects, one in Istanbul and one in Bursa. Each of the businessmen involved in these groups contributes a minimum of $1 million per year to the service projects. I also conducted focus groups with a local circle of engineers and doctors, as well as with two groups of blue collar workers. These interviews provided insights into the amounts of money contributed by individuals in various occupational groups, as well as motivations for the giving and rewards associated with involvement in the movement.

In March, 2009, I returned to Turkey with a group of sociologists of religion from the United States and Canada. For most of them, this trip was their first introduction both to Turkey and the Gülen movement. Visiting Gülen-inspired schools, a hospital and the relief agency, as well as sharing a meal in three different Muslim homes, generated a lot of remarks and discussions regarding the movement. It was helpful for me to hear fellow sociologists reflect and comment on various aspects of the movement. I was reassured that my earlier observations and conclusions were on the whole substantiated by the analyses of my professional colleagues.

What explains why the Gülen Movement has captured the commitment and enthusiasm of millions of Turks within the country as well as in the countries to which they migrate? Likewise, why is the movement attracting non-Turks in areas where Turkish migrants are living, working and studying? Whether measured in terms of numbers of members, global outreach, or commitment of members, the Gülen Movement is thriving. What explains its success? In part, these questions provide the focus of this book. Chapter 2 on "Islam and the State Throughout Turkish History" presents an overview of the history of Turkey since the late Ottoman empire to the present from the perspective of the relationships between the state and religion (i.e. Islam). This historical, political background is essential to understand the societal context in which Mr. Gülen was raised, in which he developed his ideas and to which he was responding in his sermons and writings. In Chapter 3, "Fethullah Gülen, His Life, Beliefs and the Movement he has inspired", I introduce the reader to Fethullah Gülen by describing his life story, influences on his intellectual and spiritual development, the beliefs and values he espouses and the development of the movement that he has inspired. In Chapters 3, 4 and 5 I use the lens of social movement theory, especially the insights of resource mobilization and commitment theory, to describe the many service projects that are at the heart of the movement. Chapter 4, "The Network of Local Circles," and Chapter 5, "the Turkish-Islamic Culture of Giving," with emphasis on cultural and religious concepts that are deep seated in Turkish society provide the motivation and inspiration behind the good works of the Gülen movement. These numerous service projects are supported by the volunteer labor and monetary contributions of millions of members worldwide, including both rich businessmen who are giving substantial proportions of their wealth to the movement and poor wage earners who make great sacrifices to give a few dollars each month to assist with the service projects. Chapter on "The Water for the Mill: Financing of Gülen-Inspired Service Projects" analyzes the financial support behind the movement and the consequences of giving for the commitment of members. Finally, in the last chapter ("Summary") I return to the three research questions posed in Chapter "Introduction" and summarize the major findings in the book that address these questions.

Islam and the State Throughout Turkish History

To grasp both the significance of the life and teachings of Fethullah Gülen and the depth of the fears and accusations aimed at him by his critics, it is necessary to place him in the context of Turkish history, especially as it relates to the complicated issue of religion and politics. Throughout Turkish history there has never been a complete separation of Islam and the state. However, in the new republic created by Mustafa Kemal Ataturk in 1923 one of the six pillars of the state was secularism, based on the French model of state control of religion. In this chapter, I will outline the major shifts that occurred in Turkey over the past 100 years in defining the role of Islam in state politics.

The Ottoman Empire

For most of the centuries of the Ottoman Empire (roughly 1300–1922), there was a close and symbiotic relationship between the sultans (political rulers) and the caliphs (Islamic leaders). Islam turned to the rulers for protection and the rulers often used Islam for their political legitimacy.[1] There arose an intricate relationship between Islam and the state.

The Ottoman Empire was also ruled by the Islamic law, *sharia*, which did not give equal rights to non-Muslims. The leading official religious authorities (the *ulema*) reached beyond religious affairs and dominated the educational and some of the judicial systems in the empire. The *ulema* ran the *madrasas* or Islamic schools where many of the low ranking officers in the Ottoman bureaucracy were educated.[2]

The mid-nineteenth century reforms of the Ottomans were aimed at preserving the empire at a time when military defeats were weakening the sultans.

---

[1] Balci (2007).

[2] Ibid.

H.R. Ebaugh, *The Gülen Movement: A Sociological Analysis of a Civic Movement Rooted in Moderate Islam*, DOI 10.1007/978-1-4020-9894-9_2, © Springer Science+Business Media B.V. 2010

At the same time, however, the religious authorities made up the core of opposition to the Ottoman reforms, especially the trend to disregard the *sharia* in efforts to modernize and grant equality to all citizens. Despite opposition from the *ulema*, the Ottoman rulers created European style schools with European instructors along with new courts outside the system of *sharia*. In 1850 a commercial code became the first code to be constructed outside the religious rulers' sphere of influence. Simultaneously, a new generation of young people graduated from the newly founded European-style schools and were sent to Europe for higher education. This cadre of students became the Young Ottomans who demanded further reforms and achieved them by obtaining the foundation of a constitutional monarchy and the first Ottoman constitution. When, a year later, the sultan, Abdulhamid II, dissolved the parliament and suspended the constitution, the Young Ottomans went underground and eventually evolved into the Young Turks who reappeared on the Turkish scene in the early decades of the twentieth century as the Committee of Union and Progress (CUP) to shepherd Turkey into its republican era.

Islam and the State in Early Modern Turkey

Beginning in 1913 the CUP began a series of reforms that paved the way for the complete abandonment of *sharia* and subjected the religious courts to the authority of the secular courts. In 1915 the *sharia* courts were put under the jurisdiction of the Ministry of Justice. The *ulema* was eliminated and Islam was brought under state control. The properties owned by Islamic foundations were transferred to the Ministry of Finance. In 1924 the Caliphate was abolished, the Directory of Religious Affairs was founded as a state office to take care of Islamic religious affairs and control of Islamic schools (*madrasas*) was given to the Ministry of Education. The Islamic lunar and solar calendar system was abandoned except for use in religious matters. The way was paved for the secularization that would be brought about by the founder of the new Turkish republic, Mustafa Kemal Ataturk (1881–1938).

In 1923 the Turks, led by Ataturk, by organizing resistance against the invading Greek forces supported by Western powers won sovereignty over eastern Trace and all of Anatolia and transformed the nation into the Republic of Turkey. The main goal of Ataturk was to forge a path that was very distinct from that of the Ottoman Empire, especially the creation of a secular and nationalist state run without the influence of Islam in politics. The new republican elite, with Ataturk as its leader and spokesman, favored complete modernization which they saw as an escape from backwardness and expressed as a dislike and distrust of all things associated with the ancient regime and the old ways of life. Most particularly, religion and religious institutions were suspect and deemed antithetical to contemporary civilization.[3]

---

[3] Yilmaz (2005).

Ataturk and his Kemalist followers sought to create a new Turkish nation-state founded explicitly on ethnic nationalism that would replace the multiethnic, multi-religious and Islam-oriented values of the Ottoman Empire.[4]

Being a masterful politician, Ataturk introduced his reforms slowly and initially used Islam to unite and mobilize people, especially against the invading European armies.[5] It was only in 1924 that he declared that Turkish nationalism, rather than Islam, was to be the only factor in uniting Turkish people.[6] The state used the army, schools and the media to consolidate Turkish national identity and break away from Islam and the Ottoman legacy. To achieve this and deemphasize the influence of Islam, he closed the dervish lodges and the Sufi orders, banned their ceremonies and liturgy and outlawed their dress. He denounced the *fez* as headgear of a backward people and the veil as representing the subordinate status of women. The call to prayer, *ezan*, was to be chanted in Turkish rather than Arabic and the Qur'an was also translated into Turkish and printed in Latin. In order to be more westernized and modernized, he replaced the Arabic alphabet with the Latin one and adopted the Gregorian calendar, instead of the Islamic one. He also promoted equality of women and in 1934 influenced the right for women to vote in Turkey.

In 1928 Islam was removed from the constitution as the official state religion of Turkey. While still remaining an integral part of the Turkish culture, Islam's central role in politics ended. In 1937 the principle of secularism actually replaced Islam in the Constitution.

The Secularism of Ataturk

Between 1925 and 1928 a strongly Kemalist parliament[7] enacted a series of measures to secularize public life. Ataturk believed that Turkey must leave behind its past and follow the example set by Europe. Therefore, he advocated eliminating all obstacles to creating a national, secular and western country. After achieving national independence the republic implemented a rigid secular rule by denying any role for Islam in the formation of the new polity.

The secular model that Ataturk introduced into the Republic of Turkey was that of laicism or *laicite*, the system modeled on that of Europe and France, in particular. *Laicite* expands the power of the state and restricts religion to the private sphere. It is a form of secularism that demands the exclusion of religious beliefs and practices from public life and expects the state to use its power to achieve that exclusion.

---

[4] Fuller (2008).

[5] Balci (2007); Yavuz and Esposito (2003).

[6] Yavuz (2005) says that Turkey embodies an irreconcilable paradox established during the formation of the Republic. On the one hand, the state used Islam to unify diverse ethno-linguistic groups; on the other, it defined its progressive civilizing ideology in opposition to Islam.

[7] Kemalist refers to ideas and policies promoted by Mustafa Kemal Ataturk.

Laicite is antireligious and seeks to control or eliminate religion unlike the model of Anglo-American secularism that seeks to protect religions from state intervention and encourages faith-based social networking to consolidate civil society.[8] Turkish secularism is based on the notion of transforming society through the power of the state by eliminating religion from the public sphere. In fact, in the system of *laicite* any attempt to use religious discourse in public debate, even in the Turkish parliament, can be used to ban that party or individual.

Laicism became the basic principle of the Kemalist endeavor of building a nation-state in which religion was relegated to the private realm and controlled by the state. In the Fourth Congress of the People's Republican Party in 1935, Mustafa Kemal (popularly known as Ataturk), codified his ideas and goals as "Kemalism," which consisted of six principles to guide the party and the nation: nationalism, secularism, republicanism, statism, reformism and populism. These principles were informed by the dominant European ideologies at the time that perceived modernization as Westernization. The ideology and practice of Kemalism eliminated class, ethnic and religious sources of conflict by creating a classless, nationalistic (i.e. Turkish) and secular society, that is, devoid of any religious sign or practice in the public sphere. Moreover, with the influence of French positivism and laicism strong among the new leadership, the Kemalist's only legitimate agent of change was the state itself. The nation and state were seen as one and the same and all religion, and Islam in particular, was excluded from the public realm. Any form of civil unrest or popular protest was a source of suspicion and worry to the state.[9]

Kemalist laicism placed absolute faith in science and positivism and prioritized the restructuring of society according to these principles. Such a policy, therefore, prevented religious influence in the spheres of education, economics, family, dress code and politics. Secularism in this context meant excessive state penetration into everyday life and the exclusion of ethnic and religious differences. The Turkish republic established the Directorate of Religious Affairs to administer and regulate people's religious needs and affairs in the public sphere. It thereby banned all civil society-based religious networks. In 1937 these principles were incorporated into the constitution as basic principles of the state. The ideology and political system that resulted from these principles was and still is known as "Kemalism."[10]

Kemalism became the ideology of eliminating class, ethnic and religious sources of conflict by seeking to create a classless, Turkish and secular homogenized society. Thus, fear of differences became the guiding principle of the Kemalist state. Moreover, Kemalists saw change as legitimate only when it is carried out by the state itself. Therefore, any form of bottom-up modernization of civil society was a source of suspicion and worry, especially when it was motivated by religious concerns which were a threat to the secular state.[11]

---

[8] Yavuz and Esposito (2003).

[9] Ibid.

[10] Cetin (2009).

[11] Yavuz and Esposito (2003).

The principle of *laicism* or secularism was based on the French model of *laicism* in which religion is placed under the control of the state and official religious expressions are removed from public life. In 1801 the Catholic Church in France under Napoleon Bonaparte signed a Concordat that brought the state control over the church. According to the Concordat, the Vatican agreed that bishops could be nominated by the French state and all priests assigned and paid by the state. Turkish secularism, while based on French *laicism*, went even further by establishing total control of the state over religion. Not only were imams placed by the state as civil employees, but even the content of their Friday sermons was determined by the state, control that continues into modern day Turkey.

Secularism in the Kemalist context meant state penetration into everyday life and the exclusion of ethnic, religious or regional differences. Yavuz and Esposito argue that "Contrary to its aims, the Kemalist project of nationalism and secularism actually helped to construct an oppositional and ideologized Islam. Thus, religious revival became the internal dialectic of Kemalist ideology."[12] Fear of differences, especially religious differences, became a guiding principle of the Kemalist state and seen as a threat to the state.

The system of *laicite* (or *laicism*) dominated Turkish politics during the Republican Public Party years (1923–1950), years in which a single party ruled the country. The underlying philosophy was that the state knew best what was in the best interest of the people and that the RPP was protecting Islam from the influence of foreign languages and cultures.[13]

The Multi-party System in Turkey

Turkey's shift to a multi-party political system in 1946 when the Democratic Party was founded constituted a turning point in Turkey's political history, including the role of Islam in the Turkish state. By this time Islam was under the control of the state but remained an effective social and moral force in Turkey. The Democratic Party criticized the RPP's total control over Islam. In order to pacify the DP the Prime Minister began to soften policies on Islam, including the addition of courses on Islam to the educational curriculum. When the DP party was elected to office in 1950, it maintained a similar approach to secularism even though it allowed a return to Arabic for the call to prayer, removed obstacles prohibiting religious practice and teaching, and built new mosques. However, it opposed political Islam and challenges to the secular nature of the state.

The DP supported a change in the Turkish penal code introduced by the previous administration, the famous Article 163, that any movement that aims to change

---

[12] Yavuz and Esposito (2003).

[13] Balci (2008).

the social, economic, political and judicial system based even partially on religious principles and beliefs would be penalized. This article reinforced state control of religion and assured that no Islamic movement would emerge to challenge that control. The DP carried Article 163 even further in 1953 by introducing penalties for any person or group that would use religion for personal or political gain. This law, therefore, extended state control over religion and gave the state power to silence any protest based on religious teachings.

A military coup in 1960 overthrew the DP party and after the coup the Justice Party (JP) became the successor of the Democratic Party. Necmettin Erbakan wanted to run for office under the Democratic Party but was refused by the party leader, Suleyman Demirel. Erbakan, who became a major political and intellectual figure in Turkish history, was elected to parliament in 1969. It is often said that he "redefined the role of Islam in Turkish politics."[14] He aimed to unite Islamic groups under his political leadership by creating change in the system through the electoral process. Because of his Islamic leanings and teachings, he was banned from politics under Article 163 for five years. However, by the late 1960s, Turkey like most of the Islamic world, was being threatened with the ideology of socialism. One alternative to stop the rise of socialism was Islam. Even the United States, as part of its Cold War policy of containment, hoped to stop socialism and communism with the help of "an Islamic green belt" which included Turkey, Iran, Pakistan, Afghanistan, Indonesia and Malaysia, all Islamic countries. Islam was seen as an anti-dote to socialism and the Islamic world was discovering a new role for Islam in politics. And Erbakan was a major spokesman for the rising importance of Islam in world politics.

Erbakan consistently argued that he was not against secularism but against the way that secularism was practiced in Turkey. He wanted a redefinition of secularism to allow for the free practice of religion and he argued for change in the second article of the Turkish constitution which defines the secular nature of the state and can be used to attack religion at the will of the state.

In the elections of 1965 the AP party (an extension of the previous Democratic Party) came into power with Demirel as prime minister. Demirel was sympathetic to practicing Muslims and himself attended Friday prayer. Eight years later the AP party lost in the elections to the CHP (the Peoples' Party) with Ecevit elected as prime minister. Ecevit maintained that people do need religion and that religion can fuel development.

The military coup of 1980 brought the newly elected Motherland Party (MP) to power under the leadership of Turgut Ozal who emphasized Islamic education and morality as a force against socialism. Ozal supported the ideology of Turkish–Islamic Synthesis (TIS) which combines Islamic values with Turkish nationalism. TIS embraced Islam as a source of morality but rejected political Islam.[15] This

---

[14] Balci (2007).

[15] Ibid.

philosophy also presented Islam as compatible with nationalism, democracy, Kemalism and capitalism. It was under Ozal's administration that Turkey moved to a capitalist economic system and began to introduce democratic reforms. The infamous Article 163 of the Turkish penal code was removed as part of the democratization process. Likewise, the economic liberalization and growth of the Ozal period allowed the creation of a dynamic entrepreneurial class and opportunity for the existence of independent newspapers and television channels which could not be silenced by a political elite.[16] Ozal's Motherland Party combined a globally-oriented economic program with conservative social values.

It was under President Ozal that economic policy became a driving force in Turkish foreign policy. He stressed an export oriented program that opened the country to foreign investment and allowed the entrepreneurial skills of the Turkish businessmen to blossom. Subsequently, the collapse of the Soviet Union opened up new economic options for Turkey in the newly independent republics of the former Soviet Union, especially in the important energy field.[17]

Ozal argued that restrictions on freedom of conscience breed fanaticism not the other way around. Seeking to combat communism with Islamic ideals, he required compulsory instruction in Islam in all schools.[18] The members of parliament and the cabinet were visible in attendance at mosques. The headscarf was allowed in public, based on citizens' civil liberties that were guaranteed in the constitution. Opponents of the headscarf argued that Ataturk had made it the most famous symbol of the Islamic order and that to allow it in public was a direct threat directed against the secular state guaranteed by the constitution.[19]

Ozal's government also passed a law to allow university students to wear headscarves but the Turkish constitutional court reversed this decision. However, many university students continued to wear headscarves. The headscarf issue remains a major source of conflict between conservative and radical secularist groups in Turkey. While the radical secularists regard wearing the scarf as anti-secular and anti-Kemalist, liberal secularists and conservatives regard it as a basic human right.

The headscarf issue reflected one of the major impacts of Ozal's neoliberal policies, that is, the expansion of Islam in public spaces. This resulted in the pluralization of the religious sphere and to the expansion of religious networks in the economy, the media and charitable endeavors. The deregulation of broadcasting, for example, has empowered Islamic voices such as those in the Gülen movement to express themselves on diverse radio stations and television channels and in

---

[16] Ibid.

[17] Fuller (2008).

[18] Compulsory instruction in Islam was included in the curriculum by the head of the 1980 military coup, Kenan Evren, and Ozal merely continued the practice.

[19] There were also arguments citing the fact that both Ataturk's mother and wife wore the headscarf.

newspapers and magazines. These new spaces created under the Ozal administration have served to empower Islamic groups in Turkey, including those inspired by Mr. Gülen.[20]

With the liberalization and economic diversification of Turkey the religious and ethnic publics have gradually been integrated into the public sphere and have gained informal power and influence. A major structure by which this has happened is through the *dershanes*, the meeting circles that engage in conversation, inspirational readings and prayer and provide social spaces for socialization, discussion and networking. One outcome of these circles is to create new communication opportunities and a counter public in which being a devout Muslim is promoted. In this manner, the construction of a new religious consciousness is created, along with a sense of social responsibility. A major impact of these reading circles on social and political life, therefore, is that religious participation spilled over to other social spheres by offering people ties, networks and opportunities to build civic associations.[21]

While Erbakan had been banned from politics for ten years, his followers founded the Welfare Party (WP, known as the Refah Party in Turkish or RP) and were elected into parliament in 1991. Five years later he was elected prime minister of Turkey. Erbakan was an avowedly practicing Muslim who had long advocated a stronger role for Islam in the political arena. With his election, an extended public debate about the role of religion in politics and the meaning of "political Islam" in republicanism began.[22] He praised Iran for resisting the West and pledged to remove Turkey from NATO, to set up an Islamic NATO, an Islamic UN, an Islamic version of the EU and an Islamic currency.[23] In addition, the Welfare Party articulated a vision of democracy in Turkey through the use of a commonly understood religious idiom, the traditional values of Islamic values and morality.[24] This rhetoric was praised by the more conservative, religious segments of Turkish society and strongly opposed by the secularists who feared an Islamic state. Erbakan also made a series of visits to Muslim countries, an action that drew criticism from the secularists.

In 1997 a top-level military commission, known as the "Western Working Group", launched an investigation into the Welfare Party. The result was a statement issued by the National Security Council (NSC), which saw itself as a guardian of the Kemalist reforms and especially secularism, that said that "destructive and separatist groups are seeking to weaken our democracy and legal system by blurring the distinction between the secular and the anti-secular."[25] As a result of the

---

[20] Yavuz and Esposito (2003).

[21] Yavuz (2003).

[22] Cetin (2010).

[23] Mason (2000); Howard (2001).

[24] Cetin (2010).

[25] Howard (2001); Howe (2000).

report of the working group promoted by the NSC, Erbakan's government was forced to resign in what was called a "post-modern coup" and Erbakan, along with other political leaders in the party, were banned from office for five years and the party was closed.

The NSC outlined an 18 point plan that would have to be agreed upon before it would support a new government. This plan aimed to reduce the influence of Islam in Turkey and included proposals that enforced a ban on certain faith communities and religious organizations, the purging of "reactionary" personnel from governmental positions, tighter restrictions on "politically symbolic garments like women's head scarves" and the purging of military officers for so-called Islamic activities and sympathies.[26] Some analysts maintain that since the military coup of 1980, nothing has been as decisive in Turkish political life as these actions of the NSC in February, 1997, because the army affirmed its supremacy over political life in Turkey.[27] In 1998 the Constitutional Court closed the Welfare Party "because of actions against the principles of the secular republic." Members of the ousted party formed a successor party, the Virtue Party (VP) which subsequently became the largest party in the Parliament.

In 1998 Mesut Yilmaz, the leader of the Motherland Party, formed a new government and became prime minister of Turkey and pushed ahead the "February 28 Process" whose aim was to limit Islamic influence in public life. He put restrictions on admission to Imam-Hatip Schools and instructed the Ministry of Education to enforce regulations banning headscarves from schools, universities and public places. The police detained 20 leading Muslim businessmen on charges that they had provided funding for Islamic activities. A chief prosecutor in Ankara asked for the closure of MUSIAD, the independent Industrialists' and Businessmen's Association that had "religious" overtones.

In the midst of investigations of political corruption and ties to organized crime, in 1998 Yilmaz's government collapsed. Ecevit, head of the Democratic Left Party (DLP) became prime minister. The government was effective in bringing about much-needed economic reform, instituting human rights legislation and bringing Turkey closer to acceptance into the European Union. A series of economic shocks lead to new elections in 2002 and brought into power the religiously conservative Justice and Development Party (AKP) established by Tayyip Erdogan, with 34% of the popular vote. In 2007 the AKP again won the elections with an even larger majority vote (46%) than in the previous election and elected Abdullah Gul as president and Erdogan as prime minister.

The AKP portrays itself as a moderate, conservative, pro-Western party that advocates a liberal market economy and Turkish membership in the EU. Influential business publications such as *The Economist* consider the AKP party's government the most successful in Turkey in decades.[28] Fuller, former vice chairman of

---

[26] Cetin (2010).

[27] Aras and Bacik (2000).

[28] *The Economist* (05-03-20).

the National Intelligence Council at the CIA, maintains that Turkey has produced two dynamic Islamic movements that have significant importance not only for Turkey but also for contemporary Islam in general: the political JDP party and the large apolitical communitarian movement of Fethullah Gülen.[29] The AKP pledged to respect religious belief and to support moral values, but within the context of a secular state. For the AKP, secularism meant no state interference in religious practice, a stance also supported by Mr. Gülen and his supporters. In the AKP's vision, religion remained the most important human institution, creating a moral and social order, but religious institutions could best be maintained in a climate of religious freedom.[30]

While critics often accuse the party of harboring a hidden Islamic agenda, Erdogan maintains that the AKP is not a political party with a religious axis but one pushing for democratic and economic reforms in addition to stressing moral values.[31] Erdogan sought to temper his party's Islamic image by building a broad-reaching coalition with center-right parties and by supporting Turkey's bid to join the EU. Despite the party's statements, the AKP has brought on many changes that can be interpreted as being non-secular or rooted in Islam. The party has been accused of placing anti-secular individuals in government offices and of awarding government contracts to companies and individuals who are more religiously oriented. In 2007 AKP passed a bill lifting the headscarf ban in all universities. These actions were criticized by the secular parties and lead to the 2008 indictments filed with the Constitutional Court of Turkey calling for the closing of the AKP party. The justification was that the AKP party had become a "hotbed of anti-secular activities" and hence was violating the constitution of Turkey. On July 30, 2008, the Constitutional Court gave its verdict. The indictment to disband the AKP failed by one vote (five in favor and six against).[32]

As this brief history demonstrates, issues regarding the relationship between Islam and the state have dominated Turkish politics since the birth of the Turkish Republic in 1923 and even prior in the latter decades of the Ottoman Empire. No single issue has been as powerful or contentious on the Turkish political scene and continues to dominate electoral, legal and judicial affairs in that country. It is in the context of this Turkish history that Fethullah Gülen was educated, developed his ideas and religious training, was an imam and famous preacher, launched the movement that is now international and thriving globally and draws criticism from those secularists who fear that Mr. Gülen is amassing a strong following with the goal of eventually creating an Islamist state in Turkey.

---

[29] Fuller (2008).
[30] Mecham (2004).
[31] *Turkish Daily News* (07-22-2007).
[32] *Hurriyet* (07-30-2008).

Fethullah Gülen: His Life, Beliefs and the Movement That He Inspires

Fethullah Gülen's early upbringing in a small village in southeastern Turkey, his early education and exposure to the ideas of Said Nursi, his later participation in Nursi reading circles and his increasing fame as a preacher in Turkey occurred within the context of Turkish history described in the previous chapter. In addition to his training in classical Islamic sciences, he is very much a product of his Turkish nationality and the political events that influenced his six or so decades as a Turkish citizen. In this chapter, I first introduce the reader to those aspects of Mr. Gülen's early life that formed his later ideas and plans of action. Secondly, I discuss the major beliefs, convictions and priorities that guided both his early and later teachings. Thirdly, I trace the origins of the Gülen movement in Turkey and then its spread to the former Soviet Union countries and ultimately world-wide.

The Life Story of Fethullah Gülen

His Early Years

Fethullah Gülen was born in 1941 in a small farming village near Erzurum in eastern Turkey. Ezurum was known to be culturally conservative and to have a very pious population. Although there were few opportunities for a general secular education for Turkish people at this time, Mr. Gülen's parents sent him to the nearest state primary school for three years. When he completed his primary years, his father, an imam,[1] was assigned by the state to a mosque in another town where there were no secondary schools. Mr. Gülen, therefore, was forced to abandon his formal schooling in the middle of his elementary school years and began receiving an informal education, primarily from his father.

---

[1] An imam is an Islamic leader, often the leader of a mosque and/or Islamic community, who leads the prayer during Islamic gatherings. Imams are assigned to specific mosques by the state.

H.R. Ebaugh, *The Gülen Movement: A Sociological Analysis of a Civic Movement Rooted in Moderate Islam*, DOI 10.1007/978-1-4020-9894-9_3,
© Springer Science+Business Media B.V. 2010

Mr. Gülen's father, from whom he learned basic elements of Islam as well as some Arabic and Persian, was a scholar as well as an imam. Mr. Gülen remembers him as a person who enjoyed reading books and constantly read the Qur'an, meditated daily on Prophet Muhammad and his Companions and recited religious poetry. He instilled this love of learning and love for the Prophet and his companions in his son.[2]

Mr. Gülen describes his early childhood home as a "guesthouse for all knowledgeable and spiritually evolved people in the region." His father especially welcomed scholars into his home with whom he could discuss religious issues. In Mr. Gülen's words, "Guests, especially scholars, were frequent in our house. We paid great attention to host them. During my childhood and youth, I never sat with my peers or age group; instead, I was always with elder people and listened to them talk about things of mind and heart."[3] Because of this early contact with scholars and religious thinkers, Mr. Gülen was raised in a circle of people who were constantly exploring spirituality and its place in the modernizing world.

Mr. Gülen's mother, who secretly taught the Qur'an to the girls of the village,[4] also instructed him as did his grandfather who was one of his early heroes. A decade earlier, Ataturk and the Kemalist government had established the six Kemalist principles, including nationalism and secularism. Although mosques and prayer were allowed by the secularist government, at this time in Turkish history all other forms of religious instruction and practice had been banned. Nevertheless, Mr. Gülen's parents, like many other Turkish people, continued in the Turkish Islamic tradition to make sure that he learned the Qur'an and basic religious practices, including prayer.

Another influential teacher in his early years was Sheikh Muhammed Lutfi Efendi, a Sufi teacher. It was from him and other Sufi masters that Mr. Gülen was introduced to the writings of Said Nursi (1876–1960), a preacher who taught that Muslims should not reject modernity, but find inspiration in the sacred texts to engage with it.[5] Nursi had developed ideas of a modern Islam that insisted on the necessity of a significant role for religious beliefs in public life while embracing simultaneously scientific and technological developments. Nursi's writings reinterpret

---

[2] Fethullah Gülen. *Kucuk Dunyam* (My Small World). Interviewed by Latif Erdogan, *Zaman*.

[3] Ibid.

[4] Although mosques and public prayer were allowed to continue in "secularist" Turkey, at this time all other forms of religious instruction and practice had been banned, including Qur'anic schools.

[5] During the first half of his life, Nursi participated in political life in various forms. During the second half of his life, after 1920, which he calls "the new Said," he retreated to a remote corner in the province of Van and dedicated himself to the writing of what would later become the "Treatise of Light," a 6,000+ pages of thematic commentary on the Qur'an and the life of the Prophet. Until 1950 he consistently rejected involvement in politics. During the last ten years of his life he supported the Democratic Party and NATO membership of Turkey against what he saw as a grave threat of atheism and philosophical materialism from the Soviet Union and the representatives of its ideology in Turkey, the CHP.

the Qur'an in light of modern science and rationality. The goals of the Nursi movement
that arose out of his teachings are: synthesis of Islam and science; an acceptance of
democracy as the best form of government within the rule of law; raising the level
of Islamic consciousness by indicating the connection between reason and revelation; and achieving this-worldly and other-worldly salvation within a free market
and through quality education.[6] These Nursi-inspired ideas were very influential in
Mr. Gülen's early education and became the cornerstones of his later teachings
and writings.

Along with his study of Islam, Mr. Gülen also focused on educating himself in
science, philosophy, literature and history. He would stay up late at night studying
the main principles of modern sciences such as physics, chemistry, biology and
astronomy. He also read existentialist philosophers such as Camus, Sartre and
Marcuse, Western classics including Rousseau, Balzac, Dostoyevski, Pushkin,
Darwin and Tolstoy and original sources in Eastern and Western philosophy, both
Islamic and non-Islamic.[7]

His Early Years of Preaching

As a teenager, Mr. Gülen was introduced to the Nursi reading circles and subsequently became an active participant. As opposed to tarikats, or Sufi orders, groups
of such circles around the teachings of a scholar were called *cemaat*. A *cemaat* is
a specific Turkish form of Islamic self-organization that evolved after the formation
of the secular Republic in 1923 and the outlawing of the Sufi orders and the abolishment of the madrasas (classical Islamic educational institutions). The *cemaat*
phenomenon emerged from the motivational reading circles of practicing faithful
citizens in the context of the pressure from the government on any organization that
could potentially challenge the new regime politically. In the case of Nursi reading
circles, the core topic of discussion was how to respond to the demands of the
modern world with Islamic knowledge in order to make Islam compatible with
modernity. The *cemaat* had no formal membership requirements, no initiation rites
and required no specific building or room in order to convene; therefore, it was not
a Sufi order, even though Nursi was strongly influenced by the poet, Rumi, and
other Sufi masters. Rather, the *cemaat* consisted of people who shared a common
discourse and goals within the *cemaat*.[8] The more these norms were accepted and
the more a person worked for the cause of the *cemaat,* the stronger his inclusion into
the *cemaat*.[9] Fethullah Gülen was a participant in the Nur *cemaat*, an experience

---

[6] Yavuz (2003a).

[7] Eyup Can, "Fethullah Gülen Ile Ufuk Turu" (A Tour of Horizon with Fethullah Gülen) *Zaman.*
August, 1995.

[8] Agai (2005).

[9] Mardin (1989).

that greatly influenced his subsequent life and the motivational circles formed by his own listeners and readers. In fact, a key to understanding the social organization of the Gülen Movement lies in an understanding of the Nur *cemaat* in which Gülen was socialized in his early adult years.

The readers, scribes and audiences of Nursi's discourse also established *der-shanes*, or reading circles, that met in private homes, usually consisting of university students who met together regularly to read and discuss the Qur'an and other spiritual works. The *dershanes* provided "zones of religious socialization within the secular educational setting."[10] In these *dershanes* students studied the Qur'an and the works of Nursi and established close relationships among themselves. These *dershanes* served as spaces for meeting and discussions of philosophical, social and religious topics. They became the model for the dormitories and "lighthouses" that Mr. Gülen later helped to establish.

Even though Mr. Gülen did not attend state supported secondary schools but rather the informal system of *ijaza* (licenses to teach), he completed his secondary school secular education through external exams. In 1959 he also sat for and passed the state exam to become an imam and was assigned by the state to a prestigious post because his success in the exam demonstrated his profound knowledge required of imams.[11]

Erzurum, where he received his early education, was also an important center for defending Turkish nationalist ideology. It was traditionally located on a caravan route from Anatolia to Iran and became a major rail station on the Ankara–Iran route. Located as it is at the frontier of Turkey and having many immigrants from the Caucuses, the area boasted a culture that was at the forefront of protecting the Turkish Islamic frontier against attacks from the East, both from actual outside attacks and from supporters of eastern countries who lived within Turkey. Mr. Gülen, as a young man, lead the Turkish Association for Struggle Against Communism in Erzurum and later on recruited ideological support against the political threat of Iranian Islam.[12] His years in Erzurum, therefore, were crucial in forming Mr. Gülen's deep convictions in regard to Islam and nationalism. Throughout his life, Gülen valued and preached Turkish identity.

As a young man Fethullah Gülen went to another frontier city in western Turkey, Edirne, where he served as a mosque leader for four years, fulfilled his military duty, and then spent one more year at another city in the region. In Edirne, and a year later in Kirklareli, he became very influential among the educated youth and ordinary people. He organized his own evening lectures and talk series in which he emphasized morality in private and public life. In 1966 the Turkish Directorate of Religious Affairs, a state office created in the early days of the Republic to administer Islamic religious affairs, appointed Mr. Gülen to a *kestanepazari*[13] in Izmir, the

---

[10] Agai (2005).

[11] Cetin (2010).

[12] Aktay (2003).

[13] *Kestanepazari* is a dormitory and Qur'anic school where students attended regular public schools and received additional tutoring in Qur'anic recitation and Islamic sciences.

third largest city in Turkey, where he was to teach Islamic sciences and was responsible for a mosque, for a student body and boarding hall and for preaching in the Aegean region. He lived an ascetic life and for five years resided in a small shack and did not accept any wages for his services. It was during these years that Mr. Gülen's ideas on education and service to the community began to develop. Beginning in 1969 he set up meetings in coffeehouses and lectured all around the provinces and in the villages of the Aegean region.

Establishing the First Educational Projects

Mr. Gülen, together with administrators of the Kestanepazari institution and with the support of local businessmen, also organized summer camps for middle and high school students, as well as university students. These camps taught secular education courses in areas such as history and biology but also provided religious discussions on issues such as the role of Islam in public debates. Mr. Gülen often evoked the life of Muhammad and the classical period of the Ottoman empire as good examples of ways in which fidelity to the precepts of Islam promoted greatness. He argued that, if Turkey wanted again to be a great nation, it was necessary for people to live a faithful Islamic life and to recognize God in their public institutions.[14] Since state schools did not teach Islam, Mr. Gülen was afraid that the youth were not being taught the principles of Islam. The summer camps were one way to teach school-age children about their faith, along with secular subjects.

In addition to the summer camps, starting in the 1970s Mr. Gülen's listeners began to form a new *cemaat* around his teachings, similar to the Nursi-inspired *cemaat* that Mr. Gülen attended earlier. However, what drew people to Mr. Gülen's messages were his large public sermons in front of thousands of listeners and public lectures which were recorded and sold throughout the country. His listeners comprised mostly low to middle-income businessmen, with a small number of wealthy ones, and university students.[15] He attracted people who supported his ideas, not only by attending his lectures, but also with financial support and contributions of their labor. In a modification of the Nur movement *dershanes*, Mr. Gülen helped students, their parents and donors to establish "houses of light" where Islamic education was studied on the basis of Nursi's writings and his own teachings. These "houses of light" became a source for the thousands of educators who would later form the faculty of schools established after Mr. Gülen's educational philosophy. This is the stage in Mr. Gülen's career at which a group of people numbering about one hundred began to be visible as a service group, that is, a group that came together around his understanding of service to the community.[16]

---

[14] Yavuz (2003b).

[15] Kalyoncu (2008).

[16] Cetin (2009).

Aware of how the youth in Turkey were being attracted into extremist, radical ideologies, including atheistic communism and materialism, as a preacher Mr. Gülen tried to educate the youth about traditional moral values and to attract them away from what he saw as destructive and degrading ideas. This was the era in which Erbakan, a major figure in the ruling Justice Party (JP), was arguing that Islam was an alternative to socialism and was promoting a greater role for Islam in global politics. Against this political background, Fethullah Gülen also promoted Islamic ideals as an anti-dote to the radical Marxism, Leninism and Maoism that was attracting many youth in the region. He often used his own money to buy and distribute materials that countered militant atheism and communism. He saw the erosion of moral values among the youth as the causes of crime and societal conflict and was resolute to do all he could to influence the youth in what he saw as a healthier and more productive direction.

In 1970, as a result of a military coup, a number of prominent Muslims in the region who had supported religious activities and lectures for the region's youth were arrested, Mr. Gülen among them. He was held for six months without charge. He was released on the condition that he give no more public lectures. After his release, Mr. Gülen left his official post in Izmir but retained his status as a state-authorized preacher. He continued to urge donors and parents to set up student study and boarding halls throughout the Aegean region. In Izmir he organized summer camps and dormitories where university students could stay, study and develop a sense of identity as Turkish Muslims. In these dormitories, a small group of same-sex students lived together, helped one another with studies, read the Qur'an and writings of Nursi and Mr. Gülen, prayed together, and developed a powerful sense of solidarity. Students learned and inculcated Islamic values of self-sacrifice and social responsibility. The dormitories served as shelters against alcohol and drug use, premarital sexual exploits, and involvement in communist, ultra-nationalist or other radical movements. Many conservative and religious parents encouraged their children to live in the dormitories as they attended university in the big cities in Turkey.

Izmir was a city where political Islam never took hold and where the business and professional middle class came to resent the constraints of a state bureaucracy. Instead this group supported market-friendly policies and pro-Western ideas. Mr. Gülen's commitment to the free market and his encouragement to businessmen to grow their businesses, make them global and competitive and then contribute a portion of their wealth to support service projects appealed to this entrepreneurial spirit. The funding for dormitories and private schools came from local businessmen who supported Mr. Gülen's mission of educating the youth both in secular subjects and principles of morality. It was in Izmir that a powerful transnational movement began to crystallize around Mr.Gülen that today includes thousands of loose networks of like-minded individuals.

Between 1972 and 1975 Mr. Gülen held posts as a preacher in various cities in the Aegean and Marmara regions where he continued to preach and promote ideas about education and service to the community. At the time educational opportunities were scarce for ordinary Turkish people and some citizens thought that most education was infiltrated by radical political elements, both on the left and the right.

Parents whose children had passed the required entrance exams for high school and university were caught in the dilemma of wanting their children educated but fearing the highly politicized atmosphere of the schools. To address this dilemma, Mr. Gülen encouraged small business owners to set up boarding houses where students could pursue an education in an atmosphere that he hoped was removed from the politicized environment. To support these houses and opportunities for education, local people who shared Mr. Gülen's service ethic set up "bursaries," accounts that supported the activities. Again, it was local people who saw the need for quality education and were influenced by Mr. Gülen's service ethic and who stepped forward with the resources to put his ideas into action.

Over time, the students who lived in the boarding houses became major advocates of Mr. Gülen's service ideas and returned to their villages and towns to spread the word of their valuable experiences and opportunities. Armed with a good education, they became merchants, businessmen and professionals in their communities and began to join together to provide the financial support to keep the boarding houses and consequently other service projects going. At the same time, Mr. Gülen's talks and lectures were recorded on audio cassettes and distributed throughout communities in Turkey. He was the first preacher whose lectures were made available in audio and video cassettes to the general public in Turkey. Through his students' activities in their communities and the new technological channels of communication, Mr. Gülen's service discourse began to spread in Turkey.

In 1974 Mr. Gülen was posted in Manisa where he began the first university preparatory courses in an attempt to prepare ordinary Turkish children for higher education. Up until this time, it was almost exclusively the children of wealthy families who were able to go to university. By providing top notch preparatory courses, a broader swatch of middle and working class children were prepared to take the mandatory exams in order to get into universities and to succeed once there.

The Establishment of Gülen-Inspired Schools

With the neo-liberal policies of Ozal in the early 1980s and greater opportunity for the establishment of private schools, in 1982 the first two Gülen-inspired high schools opened, one in Izmir and the other in Istanbul. These were followed in the course of the next two decades by hundreds of such schools throughout Turkey and eventually to the Turkish republics of the former Soviet Union, then to other successor states of the Soviet Union, the Balkans, South Africa and finally the West. At the World Economic Forum in Davos in 2000, Prime Minister Ecevit recognized in his speech the importance of Gülen-inspired schools all over the world, and how these schools contribute to the cultures and well-being of Turkey and other countries.[17]

---

[17] Bacik and Aras (2002).

Mr. Gülen encouraged his listeners to invest in private secular elite high schools where he hoped to combine Islamic morals with secular knowledge. These schools are based on a secular curriculum approved by the state and use English for instruction. The only Islam that is formally taught in the schools is the hour that is allowed by the state for religious instruction in comparative religions with the textbook selected by the state. All the schools, as well as other Gülen-inspired institutions, are independent units administered and funded by local groups. Yet the personnel in these schools are joined in what Agai[18] calls an "educational network of virtue," based on the fact that the leading figures were socialized within the *cemaat*, participate in the *cemaat's* life and are connected to each other through the close interpersonal links created in the *cemaat*. Many of the principals and teachers in the schools, both within Turkey and outside of Turkey, come from among educators with substantial involvement in the *cemaat*. The *cemaat* makes sure that qualified and motivated people move within the network to where they are needed to serve.

In the schools, however, there are also teachers who are not participants in the Gülen movement and may never have heard of Fethullah Gülen. However, without the commitment of Gülen-inspired teachers who view their work as religious service, these quality schools would not exist. Many parents send their children to these schools because they recognize them as the best education possible for their children. As Agai remarks, Mr. Gülen managed to strengthen the influence of his *cemaat* through opening it and making it part of a larger conglomerate of educational networks. While the institutions rely on the *cemaat* for motivated teachers and financiers, Mr. Gülen aimed his ideas at a broader audience interested in education and modernization.

In 1977 at the age of 36 Fethullah Gülen was widely recognized as one of the most influential preachers in Turkey. In that year, on an occasion when the prime minister and other state dignitaries came to Friday prayer at the Blue Mosque in Istanbul, he was invited to preach.

Gülen-Inspired Media Outlets

Mr. Gülen also encouraged his followers to go into publishing as a way of spreading the importance of education and service. Again, the liberalization of the political environment and the opportunity for independent and uncensored news media introduced by President Ozal provided the context in which private publishing establishments were possible in Turkey. In 1979 a group of teachers inspired by Mr. Gülen's ideas of education established the Teachers' Foundation to support education. This Foundation began to publish its own monthly journal, *Sizinti,* which became the highest selling monthly journal in Turkey.[19] Its mission was to relate

---

[18] Agai (2005).
[19] Cetin (2010).

science and religion, to show that the two were not incompatible and that knowledge of both was essential to a successful education. Each issue of the journal carries an editorial written by Mr. Gülen. In addition, hundreds of his sermons were audio and video recorded and the series of sermons on key topics were published in the form of over 60 books, many of them becoming best sellers in Turkey. Many of these are available in translation in the major world languages, in print and electronically, through numerous websites.

Likewise, Mr. Gülen constantly encouraged the use of technological advancements as a way of educating masses and youth. In 1982, under the presidency of Mr. Ozal, the constitution introduced social reforms that allowed for more social and religious organizing. These reforms opened doors for previously restricted religious expression and led to religious revival throughout the country. As a result, in the 1980s many of Mr. Gülen's talks were recorded and distributed on videotape, thus spreading his service discourse to ever wider audiences throughout Turkey. By the late 1980s his sermons drew huge crowds in the tens of thousands, numbers unprecedented in Turkey.[20] These sermons were also videotaped and disseminated widely throughout the country.

Participants in the Gülen Movement have also established a national television station (Samanyolu Televizyonu – STV), a major news agency (Cihan Haber Ajansi – CHA), *Zaman,* an independent daily newspaper that has the largest daily circulation in Turkey and is printed in ten world languages and in local Turkish languages all over the Turkish world, several leading magazines and The Light, Inc., a publishing house.

Success is the best advertiser of opportunity and, in this case, as word spread of all that Mr. Gülen and people inspired by his message were achieving, he was invited to speak all over Turkey. Local groups were also eager to open Gülen-inspired schools in their areas. As well as teaching arts and humanities, the Gülen-inspired schools were extremely successful in preparing students for university admissions tests and for national and international science competitions in math, chemistry, biology and computer science. The success of the private schools established by the movement was, for many, a confirmation of what Mr. Gülen had always argued in his speeches and writings, namely, that one could be a pious Muslim and yet modern at the same time.

Mr. Gülen as Lightning Rod for Critics

Given Turkey's modern history as a secular republic, dating to the establishment of the Republic of Turkey by Mustafa Kemal Ataturk in 1923, and the establishment of secularism as one of the six Kemalist principles, it was almost inevitable that the

---

[20] Ibid.

visibility and growth of the movement would catch the attention and arouse fear in the secular political arena.

Beginning in 1971, with the arrest and six month imprisonment of Mr. Gülen, he was periodically accused by state authorities of threatening laicism of the official regime. In the late 1990s controversy erupted around him when a private Turkish television channel broadcast videotapes in which he was seen to be preaching struggle against the secular republic and for the need to overthrow and replace it with an Islamic state. Some of his supporters have argued that these videotapes were made from a combination of images and sound recordings sophisticatedly doctored in order to criticize and attack him.[21] In 2000 the state prosecutor, Yuksel, filed for the arrest of Mr. Gülen charging that he and his sympathizers organized a group to change the secular government and turn it into a theocratic state. After years of court appearances and appeals, in May, 2006, the case against Mr. Gülen was finally dismissed by the High Criminal Court in Ankara.

In 1999 Mr. Gülen moved to the United States to seek medical treatment for his many ills, including heart problems and diabetes. Even in the United States, he is not free of controversy. In November, 2006, Mr. Gülen filed a petition for permanent residency (known as the "green card") which would allow him to live and work legally in the country. The U.S. Citizenship and Immigration Services (USCIS) refused his request arguing that the basis he had set forth, namely, his status as "an extremely talented academic" were insufficient and unsubstantiated. Mr. Gülen's appeal was heard in a federal court in the Eastern District of Pennsylvania (where he resides) and upheld by the court that ruled that the USCIS denial was inappropriate. In October, 2008, Mr. Gülen's petition for permanent residency was finally granted by the United States government.

As the above life story demonstrates, Mr. Gülen has been an inspiration for millions of Turks worldwide who resonate with his ideas, are committed to being part of the *sohbets* (local circles) of people who have conversations around the themes in his sermons and writings and give their time and money to supporting the service projects that he inspires. On the other hand, however, are Turks who are convinced that Mr. Gülen and his followers are set on establishing a theocratic state in Turkey, leading Turkey backwards in its move toward modernization, brainwashing young people to follow their ideas and establishing a secret society devoted to Mr. Gülen and his agenda. What are the ideas, beliefs and worldview of Mr. Gülen that inspire some and lead others to fear for the future of Turkey?

[21] Weller (2006).

Major Ideas Promoted by Mr. Gülen

Building Bridges Between Islam and the West

A major focus of Mr. Gülen's teaching is the need to create bridges between the Muslim world and the West, along with the importance of synthesizing scientific and technological advances in contemporary Muslim society. He believes that just as Turks played a pivotal religious and cultural role under the Ottomans for centuries, Turkey is now poised to lead the Muslim world into the twentieth and twenty-first centuries with emphasis on tolerance, dialog, science and education. While Mr. Gülen believes that there is only one authentic Islam based on the Qur'an and the traditions of the Prophet, he recognizes the different historical, cultural and social interpretations of Islam in the modern world.[22]

Mr. Gülen defends a progressive notion of Islam in which Muslims and Muslim nations are able to engage the world with the best of science, education, philosophy, social sciences and technology. He argues that since the advent of Islam in the sixth century, it has interacted with distinct historical and cultural conditions and that Muslims lagged behind when they failed to compete in the increasingly global world in the late nineteenth century.

In order to regain a respectable role in the modern world, Mr. Gülen frequently reminds his followers of the Ottoman legacy in contemporary Turkey. He does not advocate a return of the caliphate but rather a focus on the major cultural values and practices of the Ottomans: (1) the spirit of dialog; (2) the fact that the Ottoman state was multilingual, multiethnic and multireligious; (3) respect for women; and (4) the intellectual and cultural rapprochement between Ottoman society and the West begun in the nineteenth century.[23] Mr. Gülen advocates using the Ottoman model as a basis for returning the Muslim world to the center of world civilization and for creating productive ties with the West. Because of its strategic geographical location between East and West and its democratic system of governance, he also sees Turkey as the leader in the Muslim world for bridging the East–West gap.

Mr. Gülen believes that the contemporary Muslim world faces a number of serious challenges, one of which is the absence of a true scientific mentality as evidenced in many Muslim countries, and the second of which is the absence of true dialog between the Muslim world and the West.[24] He admits that the Muslim world has been dominated and subjugated by the Western world over much of modern history. However, he feels that it is time for the Muslim world to demonstrate the positive side of Islam to the West.

---

[22]Much of the material in this section is based on interviews that Nevval Sevindi conducted with Mr. Gülen in 1997 and again in 2001, after the September 11 attacks in New York and Washington. They are published in Sevendi (2008).

[23]Abu-Rabi (2008).

[24]Ibid.

One way that Muslims begin to show the positive side of Islam is to engage in globalization and to engage and to interact with peoples all over the world. He advocates the formation of a "golden generation,"[25] that is, highly educated and responsible young people who think internationally. This new generation is encouraged to travel widely, learn several languages, study the physical and social sciences in many different educational settings and to engage actively in interfaith dialog wherever they are.

Education

The major problem in the world today, according to Mr. Gülen, is lack of knowledge which includes the production and control of knowledge, as well as acquiring existing knowledge. Producing, maintaining and disseminating knowledge can only be achieved through quality education, not by politics or force. Education, for Mr. Gülen, is the answer to becoming a productive and contributing individual in every society. No individual or society, he maintains, can reach its fullest potential without education. He sees education as the means by which people become the true beings that God created them to be; thus to be educated is life's most important task. He says:

> The main duty and purpose of human life is to seek understanding. The effort of doing so, known as education, is a perfecting process through which we earn, in the spiritual, intellectual, and physical dimensions of our beings, the rank appointed for us as the perfect pattern of creation.[26]

He sees three forms of education (i.e. science, humanities and religion) that enhance and complement one another and that need to operate together to form the complete and whole human being (Aslandogan and Cetin 2006). Mr. Gülen advocates the inculcation of ethical values along with a sound training in the secular sciences.

He sees education as requisite for social, economic and political modernization and advocates that individuals will respect democratic law and human rights only if they receive a sound education. Social justice and peace, he argues, are achieved by intellectually enlightened people with strong moral values and a sense of altruism. Mr. Gülen and those inspired by his words hope to educate a generation trained with modern knowledge as well as Islamic morals. This philosophy is the basis of the educational system in all the schools, primary, secondary and university level, that are inspired by Mr. Gülen's ideals.

---

[25] Sevendi (2008).

[26] Gülen, *Toward a Global Civilization of Love and Tolerance*, p. 202.

While advocating educational, scientific and interfaith engagement globally, Mr. Gülen insists that this does not mean accepting Westernization in its entirety. He argues that although western civilization has dominated the world for the last several centuries, and has provided the lead in science and technology, the world-view of the modern West is materialistic and lacking in focusing on other dimensions of the human being, especially the spiritual.[27] In particular, since the Enlightenment, many people have separated religion from the goals of science and consider religion outdated and a threat to scientific enquiry. Mr. Gülen insists that religion and science go hand in hand and that religion can and should play a role in ethical, intellectual and societal realms.

In Mr. Gülen's view, science and faith are not only compatible but complementary. He sees a faith-based worldview as providing a comprehensive and sound narrative that can support and give meaning to secular learning. In his words, the best knowledge enables pupils to connect happenings in the outer world to their inner experiences.[28] He also rejects religion as blind faith and criticizes those who fail to use their reason and to explore and analyze the observable universe. Therefore, he sees the necessity of reconciling faith and reason rather than disparaging either of them.

Mr. Gülen's criticisms of the traditional *madrasas* (religious schools) and *takyas* (traditional Islamic institutions of education) is that they do not meet the demands of modern life as they lack the methods and tools for preparing students to make positive contributions to the modern world because of their failure to integrate science and technology into their traditional curricula. He also criticizes the secular schools for failing to convey spiritual and ethical values to students, even if they are well equipped to teach science and technology. To resolve this, Mr. Gülen proposes an educational system that integrates scientific knowledge with ethical values.[29]

Mr. Gülen sees scientific education and Islamic education as compatible and complementary. Although he was educated in traditional Islamic institutions, he urged his listeners to open modern schools rather than traditional *madrasas*. He even advised opening schools instead of mosques. He advocates educating the young generation in Islamic knowledge through informal publications, sermons and within the family rather than through formal curricula in schools.[30]

Mr. Gülen insists that the schools inspired by the movement avoid politicization. Despite being approached by various political party leaders for endorsement, he has always maintained a non-partisan stance and strongly encourages his followers to remain out of direct involvement in politics. He argues that Turkey is already suffering from various forms of division and that education should remain an island of unity and not tainted by political ambitions.[31]

---

[27] Carroll (2007).

[28] Gülen (1998) pp. 99–100.

[29] Michel (2005).

[30] Kuru (2003).

[31] Aslandogan and Cetin (2006).

Financing the Service Projects in the Spirit of Giving and Service

To accomplish the educational projects that Mr. Gülen envisioned required human and financial resources. Teachers and principals were needed who were dedicated and committed to quality education and who were willing to make sacrifices to enhance the education of their students. Parents had to be willing to work with teachers and school administrators for common educational goals. And to achieve these goals philanthropic giving through the establishment of charitable trusts was necessary. Mr. Gülen, therefore, in the early days of the movement began to talk to people from all strata of society in Turkey. He visited groups anywhere he could find them, in cafes, in mosques, in homes throughout small villages, towns and cities throughout Turkey. Regardless of who he was addressing, his message was the same: sound education in top quality schools and to achieve this, the necessity of altruistic service and financial contributions.[32]

He constantly encouraged the social elite and community leaders, wealthy industrialists and small businessmen alike, to support quality education. With donations from these individuals, educational trusts were established to support hundreds of schools, both in Turkey and abroad.

In his sermons and appeals, he turned to ideas and values common in many religious traditions: duty, moral obligation, disinterested contributions and altruistic services.[33] As Sevindi shows, Mr. Gülen genuinely believed in and encouraged free enterprise.[34] He preached that believers must be wealthy and grow their businesses as much as possible, especially globally which he sees as the economic future of the world. A portion of the accumulated wealth, then, should be used to support the many educational projects that would work against ignorance, poverty and immorality. Mr. Gülen continuously argued that a strong free market is necessary to produce economic wealth, which in turn, can support a modern educational system which eventually will empower Muslims and the Turkish state.[35]

In the 1980s, under the leadership of President Ozal, Turkey's economic liberalization gave rise to a new entrepreneurial class who accrued wealth by investing in businesses and capital ventures both in Turkey and internationally. Many of these businessmen were attracted to Mr. Gülen's ideas of entrepreneurialism and wealth accumulation, along with a social and religious responsibility to support service projects, especially in terms of quality education, projects that would contribute to the enhancement of education among Turkish youth. And along with education in the secular subjects in Gülen-inspired schools would come moral education and the development of a strong Turkish/Muslim identity.

---

[32] Cetin (2010).

[33] Gülen (2005).

[34] Sevendi (2008).

[35] Yavuz (2003).

Mr. Gülen encouraged the new class of business owners initially to sponsor dormitories where students could stay and study together under the tutelage of dedicated teachers. The second step that he promoted was to finance college-preparatory courses to prepare students for the mandatory college entrance exam. Finally, he encouraged the financing of secular private schools established within the state's framework of education.

Mr. Gülen preached that everyone had a role to play in bringing about top notch schools in Turkey. Those who were able and motivated to do so were called upon to be administrators and teachers in the schools. Those who were owners of businesses and engaged in professional jobs should grow their wealth as much as possible in order to support the educational projects financially. Believers in Turkey and abroad must be wealthy, not just for their own benefit, but in order to support worthwhile service projects.[36] He urged businessmen to combine their resources and energies into charitable trusts in which no one benefits from what the institutions earn except the students themselves. For many businessmen building a school is the modern equivalent of building a mosque.[37]

While he, himself, remained materially poor, his asceticism and altruistic goals motivated teachers, parents and sponsors to contribute to the common good in whatever ways they were able. Apart from motivating people to donate money, Mr. Gülen remained distanced from the financial management of all institutions related to the movement. Instead, he encouraged the sponsors of these institutions to actively oversee the use of their monies. This built great trust in Mr. Gülen's honesty and integrity.[38]

Mr. Gülen often makes reference to what Ali, the fourth caliph after Muhammed, said, "all human beings are one's brothers and sisters. Muslims are one's brothers and sisters in religion, while non-Muslims are one's brothers and sisters in humanity … Human beings are the most honorable of creatures. Those who want to increase their honor should serve this honorable creature."[39] And, for Mr. Gülen, the provision of a good education through altruistic services and charitable trusts is one of the most honorable ways to show respect and reverence for fellow human beings. Work becomes an act of service of God even if only a portion of one's earnings is given to a service cause. Educational work and the support of education are particularly endowed with high Islamic value.

As we show in Chapter 5 "The Turkish–Islamic Culture of Giving", Mr. Gülen's ideas of service revived the philanthropic dynamics, altruism and benevolence that are deeply embedded in Turkish culture and filled a gap left by government policies. He transformed people's minds by bringing a new understanding of religion, science, secularism, social and educational services. He asserted that Turkey, as well as

---

[36] Sevendi (2008).

[37] Cetin (2010).

[38] Woodhall (2005).

[39] Unal and Williams (2000).

all humanity, needs more tolerant and altruistic individuals with magnanimous hearts and open minds that respect free thinking, that are open to science and scientific research, and that can perceive the harmony between the Divine laws of the universe and life.

Interfaith and Intercultural Dialog

Mr. Gülen, in his emphasis upon interfaith and intercultural dialog, often refers to the harmonious inter-religious relationships that existed in the Ottoman Empire. The Empire was composed not only of Muslims, but of many Christians and Jews as well as some Zoroastrians. Until the emergence of modern national states, these religious groups lived together peacefully and productively throughout the Ottoman times. This peaceful coexistence was promoted by many of the Turkish Sufi masters who espoused ideas of inter-religious tolerance.[40] Mr. Gülen studied many of these Sufi masters and was, no doubt, influenced by them in his insistence on the importance of dialog among these faith communities.

Concepts of compassion and love are central concepts in Mr. Gülen's teachings. He continuously advocates tolerance and forgiveness as central Islamic values that are rooted in humility. He teaches that people who believe in their own superiority will never engage in true dialog. Rather, the one who is humble will be more likely to dialog with others in an open and meaningful fashion. Mr. Gülen demonstrated his own humility when he met with Pope John Paul II in February 1998. After the meeting he was criticized by a group of young Islamists who argued that he should not have humiliated himself by going to the Vatican and meeting with the Pope. Mr. Gülen responded by saying that humility is an attribute of Muslims and that dialog with people of other religious traditions is an integral part of Islam. He reiterated that humility is essential to true dialog and that people should not think of their own superiority but instead should be humble before those of other religious traditions.[41] Rather, he perceives all humans as servants of God regardless of their ethnic, national or religious background. He quotes the Prophet as saying that there is no superiority of Arabs or non-Arabs, and of non-Arabs over Arabs. Rather, the religion of Islam gives the same value to all humans and calls them servants of the Most Compassionate One.

Mr. Gülen also asks Muslims not to make Islam an ideology which has the danger of bringing it into the political arena, an action that prevents Muslims from entering dialog with people of other faiths. Ideologies, he says, are divisive rather than uniting. He sees Islam as a religion and should not be a means of partisanship, national hatreds or feelings of enmity between people.[42] He also exemplified his

---

[40] Saritoprak and Griffith (2005).

[41] Saritoprak and Griffith (2005).

[42] Ibid., p. 337.

convictions by establishing good relationships with minority leaders in Turkey. In the late 1980s, he initiated dialog with the Greek Orthodox Patriarch Bartholomew to try to ameliorate Greeks in Turkey who were often criticized by Turkish politicians.[43] Mr. Gülen also, in the face of much opposition, worked to set up a high school in Yerevan, the capital of Armenia.[44]

The above actions of Mr. Gülen also demonstrates his insistence on inter-civilization dialog and educational advancements, along with interfaith dialog. In his words, "Our ongoing activities are for the good of all humanity. They should not be considered limited to our own country, Turkey."[45] Following this advice from Mr. Gülen, Turkish businessmen and educators have expanded schools and hospitals far beyond the borders of Turkey.

Mr. Gülen frequently reiterates the fact that inter-religious dialog is not a luxury but has become a necessity in today's global world. He recognizes that the pluralities of the contemporary world will continue to exist and present a greater and greater challenge as the world becomes a global village. In his words:

> Different beliefs, races, customs and traditions will continue to cohabit in this village. Each individual is like a unique realm unto themselves; therefore the desire for all humanity to be similar to one another is nothing more than wishing for the impossible. For this reason, the peace of this (global) village lies in respecting these differences, considering these differences to be part of our nature and in ensuring that people appreciate these differences. Otherwise, it is unavoidable that the world will devour itself in a web of conflicts, disputes, fights, and the bloodiest of wars, thus preparing the way for its own end.[46]

In the same treatise he says:

> Islam, Christianity and Judaism all come from the same root, have almost the same essentials and are nourished from the same source. Although they have lived as rival religions for centuries, the common points between them and their shared responsibility to build a happy world for all of the creatures of God make interfaith dialog among them necessary. This dialog has now expanded to include the religions of Asia and other areas.[47]

Since retiring from formal preaching and teaching, much of Mr. Gülen's efforts are concentrated on establishing dialog among the various cultures, religions and ethnic

---

[43] The Greek–Turkish War of 1919–1922 was launched because the Western Allies had promised Greece territorial gains in the Ottoman Empire. It was fought between Greece and the Turkish revolutionaries that would later establish the Republic of Turkey and ended with Greece returning to its pre-war borders and engaging in a population exchange with Turkey under provisions of the Treaty of Lausanne.

[44] Relationships between Turkey and its neighboring country of Armenia have been strained since the end of WWI (1915) when intense fighting occurred between the two countries. Armenians maintain that Turkey effected a "genocide" of over one million people; Turks maintain that similar numbers of Turks died in the conflicts that ended the war and that the war deaths on both sides were outcomes of fighting on both sides.

[45] Fethullah Gülen (1993).

[46] Gülen (2004) pp. 249–250.

[47] Gülen (2004) p. 23.

groups of Turkey and throughout the world. He does this through his intermittent visits with people of varying backgrounds who come to see him in his home in Pennsylvania, through his webcasts and by means of his regular inspirational pieces in *Zaman* and many other news outlets. He continues to be called, with great respect as well as affection, *Hocaefendi*, esteemed teacher, by his listeners and readers.

Islam Cannot Promote or Tolerate Terrorism

On September 12, 2001, Mr. Gülen bought an entire page in the *New York Times* to express condemnation of the previous day's terrorist attacks and to assert that terrorism is incompatible with the teachings of the Prophet and the religion of Islam. Again, on September 21, 2001, he expressed his position in the *Washington Post* in the following words:

> We condemn in the strongest of terms the latest terrorist attack on the United States of America, and feel the pain of the American people at the bottom of our hearts. Islam abhors acts of terror. A religion that professes 'He who unjustly kills one man kills the whole of humanity,' cannot condone the senseless killing of thousands. Our thoughts and prayers go out to the victims and their loved ones.

In a subsequent essay, he went even further to state clearly that Islam does not approve of terrorism in any form and that Islam cannot be used to achieve any Islamic goal. He used a phrase that was heard repeatedly by his followers in the years following 9/11: "No terrorist can be a Muslim and no real Muslim can be a terrorist."

Mr. Gülen also pleaded with the United States not to retaliate with the type of force that would injure innocent masses in order to punish a few guilty people. He warned that such actions would only strengthen the terrorists by feeding any existing resentment and by giving birth to more terrorists and more violence.[48]

Mr. Gülen also criticizes Muslim leaders who use Islam for their own interests and power. He says that some religious leaders and "immature Muslims" use fundamentalist interpretations of Islam to engage people in struggles that serve their own purposes. In Islam, he says, just as a goal must be legitimate so must all the means employed to reach that goal. Thus, a person cannot attain heaven by murdering another person. An individual who accepts Islam will never knowingly take part in terrorism.

Mr. Gülen insists that many young people have lost their spirituality and that some leaders take advantage of this by recruiting these disaffected youth into terrorist activities and exploiting them. He goes so far as to say that these leaders have "drugged them" by manipulating their ideas and commitments.[49] The major way to

---

[48]Ibid., p. 262.
[49]Interview with Gülen, Saritoprak (2005) p. 466.

counter these activities, for Mr. Gülen, is to provide quality education that will serve as an alternative for potential youthful recruits.

Education is the most direct and powerful anti-dote to terrorism, in Mr. Gülen's framework. He asserts that the fundamental principles of religion are totally against the political and ideological acts and interpretations that underlie and motivate brutal acts of terrorism. These fundamental principles must be taught to Muslims and to other people as well through the education system. Providing quality educa-tion for youth will challenge them to see terrorism as destructive, immoral and an act against humanity.[50]

Relationship of State and Religion

While Mr. Gülen does not advocate establishing an Islamic political system and continuously advises his readers not to get enmeshed in politics, he believes firmly that religion should not be confined to the private sphere of the individual but that it should be part of public life. He advocates a total separation between religion and politics in contemporary Muslim societies. In his view, domination of religious affairs by the state harms Islam and hence religion must be freed from state control.

The Gülen movement was the first Islamic community ever in Turkey to openly accept the legitimacy of the secular state while asking for religious freedom under it.[51] In 1998 the Journalists and Writers Foundation, a nonprofit intercultural dialog organization associated with the Gülen movement, initiated a meeting of some of the most respected theologians and Islamic scholars in Turkey. The declaration that resulted from the gathering indicated an acceptance of the secular state that would "stand at the same distance from all beliefs and philosophies."[52]

Without doubt, Mr. Gülen has strong feelings about his national heritage and is proud of his Turkishness. He constantly refers to his Turkish roots and to the Ottoman history of Turkey and the larger Turkish world. His notion of identity is therefore shaped by the Ottoman-Islamic legacy. Due to their nationalist character-istics, Mr. Gülen's community developed its own orientation and differentiated itself from other Nursi and Islamic groups by stressing nationalism, the free market and education. He is the engine behind the construction of a "new" Islam in Turkey that is marked by the logic of a market economy and the Ottoman legacy.[53] His nationalism is inclusive and not based on blood or race but rather on shared histori-cal experiences and political realities. Hence, Mr. Gülen's community argues that

---

[50]Gülen (2005).

[51]Akyol (2008).

[52]Ibid.

[53]Yavuz (1999).

Islam is the religion of the nation and should not be reduced to being the identity of any one party. For Mr. Gülen, Islam is not a political project to be implemented but rather a repository of knowledge and practices for the development of a just and ethical society.[54]

Mr. Gülen avoids any form of confrontation with the state. Rather, his main goal is not to reorient the state in terms of Islamic precepts, but rather to stress a state that does not intervene in the free exercise of religion while taking advantage of the power of faith in combating social ills such as violence and drugs. He states that "I am always on the side of the state and the military. Without the state, there is anarchy and chaos."[55] He continuously encourages his audiences to respect the state but not to become embroiled in partisan politics. Mr. Gülen is an advocate of democratic rule and argues that democracy is the most appropriate and effective form of government in the globalizing world. He says explicitly that:

> Democracy and Islam are compatible. Ninety-five percent of Islamic rules deal with private life and the family. Only five percent deals with matters of the state, and this could be arranged only within the context of democracy. If some people are thinking something else, such as an Islamic state, this country's history and social conditions do not allow it. Democratization is an irreversible process in Turkey.[56]

He goes on to advocate that his listeners respect the government and express opposition as is done in most developed, democratic, Western countries through the vote.

Evolution of the Gülen Movement

Scholars who study social movements agree that the elements of a movement must "incubate" for awhile before it emerges into the public as a recognizable social movement.[57] Because of his preaching and recorded messages, the ideas and inspiration of Mr. Gülen were becoming well known in Turkey by the early 1980s. Increasing numbers of people were joining the Gülen-inspired *sohbets*, the local circles of people who met regularly to discuss his ideas, to initiate the dormitories and preparatory classes he suggested, to finance these and other service projects and to establish a network of informal community relationships among like-minded citizens. These networks of individuals, including businessmen with the financial resources to support the service projects, had begun to form slowly in villages and cities where Mr. Gülen preached.

---

[54] Ibid.
[55] Gülen interview in *Sabah*, January 27, 1995.
[56] Ibid.
[57] Komecoglu (1997); Della Porta and Diani (1999); Melucci (1999).

By 1980 business owners and educators inspired by Mr. Gülen had responded to the crisis in education in Turkey by setting up institutions such as student dormitories, university entrance exam courses, teacher associations, publishing houses and a journal. By the mid 1980s there were sufficient resources, including informal networks of motivated people and substantial financial contributions, to accelerate the service projects already in existence and to begin building schools and hospitals in Turkey. At this point, the media became aware of the movement and newspaper articles about the movement and its many activities catapulted it into public awareness. It is at this point that the "latent" phase of the network activities gave way to a more visible and developed phase[58] and that members began coalescing around the idea of a social movement. The public also began referring to the "Gülen schools" and "Gülen followers." Mr. Gülen himself, however, never refers to the movement as the Gülen movement or the Gülen community nor does he accept these names. Instead he prefers the movement to be called the "volunteers service" or *hizmet*, which means services for others or the movement of humans united around high human values.[59]

By the middle years of the 1980s the Gülen-inspired schools were recognized throughout Turkey as providing quality education to Turkish youth. Pupils from these schools were passing the national university entrance exam at rates far higher than the general population of youth who took them, even after attending other preparatory courses. Also, many high school students in Gülen-run schools were winning national and international science competitions. The Gülen schools and the Gülen movement behind them began to achieve broader public recognition and attracted more and more participants who saw value in the ideas expressed by the movement. It was at the point of the success of the schools that the activities motivated by Mr. Gülen's ideas of education and non-political services began to coalesce into what became known as the Gülen Movement.

The collapse of the Soviet Union in 1991 and the independence of the Turkish republics in Central Asia provided the context in which the Gülen movement became transnational. In his sermons in the late 1980s, Mr. Gülen increasingly advised his audiences to prepare to help those countries that would soon gain their independence, most of which were Turkish in origin and language. In 1992, very shortly after the Soviet Union collapsed, a group of Gülen-inspired businessmen and teachers opened the first school in Azerbaijan. That same year the first Gülen-inspired school opened in Kazakhstan and in the following two years, a further 28 schools were opened in that country. Between 1992 and 1994, participants in the movement opened schools in Kyrgyzstan, where today there are 12 high schools and one university. At the same time, 20 schools were begun in Turkmenistan.[60]

---

[58] Komecoglu (1997).

[59] Cetin (2010).

[60] Kalyoncu (2008).

While some movement participants were busy opening schools in the Turkish republics, others were opening similar schools in non-Muslim countries in Eastern Europe and the former Soviet Union, such as Bulgaria, Romania, Moldova, Ukraine and Georgia. Other volunteers were establishing schools in the Asia-Pacific countries of the Philippines, Cambodia, Australia, Indonesia, Thailand, Vietnam, Malaysia, South Korea and Japan.[61] An amazing development of the Gülen movement is that it is active not only in countries with a Turkish and Muslim heritage, but also those with Christian, Buddhist and Hindu traditions. Kalyoncu argues that one reason for this is the fact that the movement began in Turkey utilizing Islamic discourse but over time began to emphasize the secular and humanistic elements in its discourse such as quality education, empathic acceptance of others and universal ethical values. He concludes that although the movement has remained Islamic at an individual level, it is a secular social movement overall.[62]

Throughout the 1980s, members of the new Anatolian bourgeoisie who were inspired by the teachings of Mr. Gülen, began to invest in the construction of learning institutions across Turkey. In the 1990s, political and economic development in Turkey under the policies of President Ozal, as well as political events worldwide, provided more and more global routes for the expansion of businesses. The fall of the Soviet Union and the weakening of Turkish state control over information and capital flows, increased Turkish migration to Europe and global developments contributed to the transformation of the Gülen movement from a small community in Turkey to an international activist movement supported by a growing class of wealthy entrepreneurs who were committed to the ideals of the Gülen movement.[63]

By the 1990s, there is no doubt that the millions of citizens gathered around the ideas of Fethullah Gülen, along with the hundreds of service projects that they support, constituted a social movement. It constitutes the largest faith-based movement in Turkey.[64] What is surprising, however, is the fact that the movement, rooted in a Turkish Islamic identity, was then and continues to be, as active in as many non-Muslim as Muslim countries. The explanation probably lies in the fact that the infrastructure of the movement, in terms of organizational leadership, volunteers, financial donors and the inspiration behind the movement, is transported by the Turkish diaspora settling in countries all over the world as students, professionals and businessmen. Some of them deliberately migrate to establish Gülen-inspired institutions in other countries; others of them migrate for educational and/or business reasons and stay involved in the movement and its service projects once they settle in a new country. As movement supporters and participants settle all over the world and establish Gülen-related projects wherever they

---

[61] Ibid.
[62] Ibid.
[63] Kuru (2005).
[64] Fuller (2008).

are, non-Turkish people are learning about the movement and becoming involved in various ways. The result is that the Gülen movement is now global in its outreach and impact.

Summary Overview of the Gülen Movement

The Gülen movement is a civic initiative, a civil society movement that is not a governmental or state sponsored organization. It did not emerge as the result of a governmental policy nor a state ideology. It started as a faith-initiated, non-political, cultural and educational movement dedicated to providing opportunity for the new generation of youth in Turkey. It centers on individual change and education of the individual. The movement focuses on the spiritual and intellectual consciousness of the individual, seeking to form an inner self that will empower the person to effect change in society. It stresses the role that technology and new global networks can play in articulating a Muslim consciousness. The Gülen movement, therefore, differentiates itself from other Islamic groups by stressing a non-exclusivist form of Turkish nationalism, the free market, openness to globalization, progressiveness in integrating tradition with modernity and its humanistic outlook.

As a person deeply rooted in both the Islamic/Ottoman tradition and the beneficial aspects of modernity, as well, Mr. Gülen is a religious modernist and a social innovator. His audiences seek to promote the idea that Islam is not in contradiction to modernization but that education, science and technology can be used along with Islam to promote a more ethical and just society. As a result, the movement is more modern and influential than any other Islamic movement in Turkey today.[65]

The Gülen Movement sets an example in the Muslim world not only with its activities but also how it generates financial support for these activities. Usage of the basic Islamic ideals and examples from the lives of the companions of the Prophet as well as traditional, Turkish values of giving and hospitality strengthens the Gülen Movement's position and impact within the Muslim world. Even though the movement started in Turkey, in a short time it has grown in other parts of the world within non-Turkish populations, not only with educational projects but also in terms of interfaith dialogue activities.

The movement has never condoned proselytization, coercion, terrorism or violence but rather stresses mentality change of individuals through science, education, dialog and democracy. It encourages reciprocal understanding and respect and encourages voluntary commitment of individuals to sound education and altruistic contributions and services.[66]

---

[65] Fuller (2008).

[66] Komecoglu (1997); Yilmaz (2005); Weller (2005).

The informal networks of Gülen-inspired people, along with the many service projects which they support, gives rise to a sense of being together in a common cause. There is an unspoken solidarity among such people, as well as a sense of pride in the institutions connected to the Gülen movement. The result is a reciprocal and public recognition of the identity of the Gülen movement. The movement has no formal ceremonial rituals, symbols, slogans or uniform dress which identify it. Rather, participation in the movement takes the form of friendship-based circles that encourage an active role in collective action. Unlike relationships based on family or tribal relationships, those in the movement rest on the voluntary and active participation of relatively independent individuals. These friendship networks facilitate and increase an individual's willingness to get involved in service projects through his/her relationship with like-minded, similarly intentioned people. The result are numerous loose networks of people who are inspired by the ideals of Mr. Gülen and motivated to support, in whatever ways they can, the vast and varied service projects in Turkey and around the world.

Service networks operate on their own and not from a centralized organization, although they maintain links to other people in the movement through sharing information and professionalized people. Information, expertise and projects circulate through networks and bring a degree of collective identity to the whole. As networks, rather than formal organizations, the Gülen movement attracts supporters or adherents. It does not have membership or a membership registry. This explains why it is impossible to calculate the size of the Gülen movement.

The movement is an aggregate of networks concentrated around four main activities: economic enterprises, educational institutions, publications and broadcasting and religious gatherings. Individuals involved in these specific projects come and go and replace one another but the service projects continue. Therefore the continuity in the Gülen movement lies in maintaining and sustaining the service projects. The participation in service projects around a specific goal and the tangible outcomes of the projects strengthens social cohesion, trust and solidarity.

Social Organization in the Movement: The Network of Local Circles

The success of Gülen-inspired projects relies on the numerous local circles of businessmen, professionals and workers in Turkish cities, towns and rural areas. The model of the local circles arose within the *cemaat,* a type of social group that evolved in Turkey after the formation of the Republic and the outlawing of the Sufi orders and the abolishment of the *madrasas.* Practicing Muslims who wanted to preserve the Islamic heritage while adapting to modernity formed circles around scholars and intellectuals who promoted various approaches such as focusing on Qur'anic studies, the blending of religious devotion with a mild form of nationalism, or individualized spiritual practices. These groups of readers and listeners around pioneering figures were later called *cemaats,* a grassroots movement of practicing faithful Turkish people who did not want to abandon their faith tradition while embracing the modern age. Within the *cemaats* were established the *sohbets* or small groups that have no formal membership, no initiation rites, require no building to convene the group and have no public insignia or recognition of membership. Rather, they consist of people who meet regularly to read Qur'anic commentary, the prophetic tradition and Muslim scholars, to share ideas and needs of people in the group and to determine service projects that the group chooses to support financially.

Among the noteworthy scholars of the era who attracted the attention of a large number of citizens was Said Nursi, who promoted a harmony between science and reason, on the one hand, and revelation and faith on the other. While Nursi was strongly influenced by the spiritual tradition of Islam, his focus was on educating the faithful against the onslaught of philosophical naturalism and materialism. As discussed in the previous chapter, Mr. Gülen in his early adult years was an active part of a *cemaat* around Nursi's teachings and experienced the fellowship and effectiveness of this form of organization.

As Mr. Gülen's ideas caught hold in Turkey in the late 1960s and early 1970s as a result of his sermons and writings, he encouraged the *sohbet* structure as a way for those inspired by his ideas to get together and discuss the relevance of these ideas for contemporary Turkish society. The Turkish people were familiar with local circles and many of them already belonged to such circles, based on their work, neighborhoods or special interests. It was natural, therefore, for these circles

H.R. Ebaugh, *The Gülen Movement: A Sociological Analysis of a Civic Movement* 47
Rooted in Moderate Islam, DOI 10.1007/978-1-4020-9894-9_4,
© Springer Science+Business Media B.V. 2010

to focus on the ideas being preached by this imam who was drawing large crowds and inspiring new hope for the future of Turkey and especially Turkish youth.

Data in this chapter come from interviews with movement participants who are part of local circles. In the spring of 2007, Dogan Koc interviewed a local circle of 12 businessmen in Ankara, as well as an interview with a businessman in Istanbul who is in the textile business and makes a substantial contribution every year to Gülen-related projects. He also interviewed a group of supporters in Houston, Texas, that consisted mostly of graduate students.[1] In spring 2008, I conducted nine focus groups with local circles of Gülen supporters in Turkey. In Istanbul I interviewed one group consisting of eight wealthy businessmen; another local circle of 16 young professionals, mostly engineers; a group of 4 doctors and an administrator at Sema Hospital; a local circle consisting of 12 blue collar workers; and a group of women who belong to a local circle. In addition, in Bursa I met with a group of three businessmen who are major donors to Gülen-inspired schools there; a group of eight doctors at Bahar Hospital; and a circle of 13 blue collar workers who meet in local circles around Bursa. Finally, in Mudanya, a small village in the outskirts of Bursa, I interviewed a group of ten men from various occupational backgrounds, including a salesclerk, an elementary public school teacher, a retired civil servant and the owner of a well established restaurant.

In addition to these focus groups, I also conducted one on one interviews with five people who belong to local circles and make substantial monetary contributions to Gülen-inspired projects both in Turkey and abroad. These interviewees include: two journalists, a wealthy entrepreneur in the food industry who owns a major company in Turkey, the owner of a major textile company and the principal of one of the Gülen-inspired schools.

The focus groups and individual interviews are representative of movement participants in terms of social class, occupations, large and small cities, gender, age and length of time in the movement. As a result, data reflect the diversity that exists in the local circles as well as among the many individuals who are part of these circles. Analysis in this chapter is framed sociologically in terms of the organizational theories of commitment discussed in Chapter Chapter l, I present data to show that the contributions made by movement members, including wealthier sponsors, both **demonstrate** commitment to the ideals of the movement and simultaneously **generate** commitment to the movement.

Structure of the Local Circles

Local circles are typically organized in two ways: (l) according to location and neighborhoods; and (2) according to education and jobs. For example, doctors in the same general area will meet together as will dentists, lawyers, accountants,

---

[1] Data from these interviews were first described in Ebaugh and Koc (2007).

teachers, factory workers, etc. While Gülen movement participants may also belong to larger professional organizations associated with the movement that has periodic gatherings, they meet weekly or twice a week in smaller groups of about 10–12 people. In these small meetings, participants talk about a variety of things, including religion, technical work, family and any aspect of life that is raised by members. Sometimes the group reads from the Qur'an or the Prophetic tradition; on other occasions, the group may host a speaker. More frequently, the members in a given group simply come together to share their lives, whatever might be important that particular week. As one member said, "What is most important is coming together and sharing with one another. Every week I close my Friday night and tell my friends not to call me or plan anything. Meeting in my local circle is the most important event of my week."

The group of workers in Bursa meet in local circles of 20–25, once a week with newcomers to the Gülen movement and once with people who have been in the movement a longer time. As one worker said, "In our culture we have values which have been lost so we read motivational materials such as Gülen books or videos or works by Nursi or something from the Prophetic tradition." Because they are not as wealthy as the businessmen, they cannot support an entire school or ten scholarships as some businessmen do but perhaps three of them support one scholarship. In addition, the group in Bursa has created Kor-Der, an association that organizes activities in 120 townships around Bursa to spread the service message of the movement, to garner donations and to determine needs in the local villages. Therefore, while the workers' group is not able to make large donations of money, members donate many hours of time soliciting assistance from others to support service projects.

As one businessman explained,

> "Being in the same type of business means that we have a strong basis for coming together and understanding one another. We also network and refer customers among us. Then we have a basis for discussing projects that need doing in our community and how we can help with these projects. We also see the results of our efforts which encourage us to be even more generous."

In fact, helping one another to be successful in their businesses is promoted by Mr. Gülen. In 2007 Tuskon, a Gülen-inspired business association with 1,500 members, sponsored a conference in Istanbul for a thousand business owners from developing countries such as Africa and Central Asia at which they were coached in ways to grow their businesses. Assisting one another in a given industry and networking among themselves is one reason that the Gülen business community in Turkey is known as one of the richest communities in the country.[2]

Organizing on the basis of natural groups, such as professions or occupational groups, also facilitates recruitment. Groups that share strong distinctive identities and dense interpersonal networks are highly organized and hence readily mobilized. The "bloc recruitment" of preexisting solidarity groups represents the most

---

[2] Baskan (2004).

efficient form of recruitment.[3] Movements that focus on preexisting or "natural" groups and that link their vision of change to that preexisting group culture are more effective than efforts to recruit lone individuals. Individual recruitment requires greater resource investment and is much slower than bloc recruitment.

All of the local circles I visited were gender-segregated. When I inquired about women members, in each circle I was told that the circles are open to women but that the women prefer to meet by themselves and were more comfortable with other women. In the case of the engineers, for example, about 10% of women engineers meet in mixed circles. There are parallel local circles for women engineers where the remaining 90% meet. The same holds true for doctors, nurses, dentists, accountants, blue collar workers, etc. One reason for the segregation, I was told, is logistical. The women prefer to meet earlier in the day before their children are home from school activities and require their attention. Also, for safety reasons, women do not like to be out after dark when many of the male circles meet.

The issue of the role of women in the Gülen movement was raised repeatedly throughout my interviews. Critics of the movement, both in Turkey and in Houston, Texas, maintain that women in the movement are viewed and treated subserviently, are expected to fulfill the traditional roles of raising the children and taking care of the home, are encouraged to wear the headscarf, are discouraged from social interactions with men and are discouraged from public leadership roles.[4] In my interviews with women, in Turkey and in the United States, I discovered a wide array of differences among women both in their judgments of how they are treated within the movement and in observing the roles played by women in movement activities. For example, in San Antonio, Texas, a covered woman has been the spokesperson and master of ceremonies at the annual Ramadan dinner which is attended by hundreds of people from the community. This has not been the case in Houston, Texas, where a man has always lead the event and served as president of the local group. In Turkey many of my female interviewees value the fact that they are allowed to teach in the Gülen-inspired schools and hospitals while wearing the headscarf, something forbidden in the public institutions in Turkey. Many of these women find empowerment in being able to decide for themselves what to wear as well as a space in the Gülen-related institutions to exercise their individuality and abilities.[5]

---

[3] Tilly (1978); Oberschall (1973); Snow, Zurcher and Eckland-Olson (1980); McCarthy and Wolfson (1996); Melucci (1999).

[4] See the Conclusions chapter for a description of the interviews I conducted with critics of the Gülen movement.

[5] The issue of women in the Gülen movement has been understudied by academic outsiders, especially scholars also well versed in Turkish culture, who can bring a systematic and non-ideological perspective to the topic.

I interviewed in one women's local circle in the Asian part of Istanbul. The group consisted of a mixture of women from varying occupational backgrounds including one former and one current teacher in a Gülen-inspired school, a lawyer, an accountant, a secretary, a salesperson and a stay-at-home Mom. When I asked how they felt about being excluded from male circles, I was corrected in the following way, "We are not excluded. We don't want to meet with the men. We feel more comfortable meeting among ourselves. Then we can talk about what interests and concerns us which is different from that of the men."

The circles of women, I learned, operate similarly to those of the men. The groups meet every week, read from the Qur'an, the Prophetic tradition, Mr. Gülen's writings and other inspirational books. The women then discuss the topic, especially how it relates to their own lives. They also discuss their families, problems they might at home especially with their children and service projects that need their help. Those women who work outside the home make financial contributions to Gülen projects. The women also engage in *kemes,* that is, the Turkish practice of making hand-crafted articles (e.g. embroidery, crocheting, artwork, etc.) that they then sell and give the profits to projects in need of assistance.

An essential part of every local circle is supporting some needy project, either in Turkey or in another country. When asked how the group learns about needs in the community, I was told repeatedly that the Gülen-inspired community is tight-knit and people know which projects need help. Some people have been in contact with and supporting educational projects for years and know what is going on in the educational field. Others are connected to the hospitals and know what needs exist there. Still others travel outside Turkey and are aware of needs in other countries. Word circulates which projects are especially in need at a given time and people in local circles get together and decide what they can do.

In addition to financial giving throughout the year, twice throughout the year Muslims celebrate special festivals that call forth the sense of sharing with the needy. During the month of Ramadan when every practicing Muslim fasts from sunrise to sunset and makes a special effort to live a virtuous and disciplined life, there is also the requirement of sharing one's abundance with those in need. Almost without exception, Muslims around the world are particularly generous during Ramadan with their charitable contributions.

The second festival is Eid-ul-Adha, the Day of Sacrifice, that occurs right after hajj, the annual pilgrimage to Mecca that is required once in a life time for all able-bodied Muslims who can afford it. On the Day of Sacrifice Muslims sacrifice animals who have been deemed *halaal* or fit for sacrifice, in remembrance of the sacrifice that Abraham made to God. They not only eat the meat themselves but distribute it amongst their relatives, neighbors and friends and finally, one-third is given to the poor and hungry. The goal in many Muslim communities is to join together to see that no impoverished neighbor is left without sacrificial food during this day.

At the time of Eid-ul-Adha several months prior to my interviews, a group of businessmen from Bursa traveled to Darfur, Sudan, where they bought three bulls to slaughter and gave as food to poor people there. They also met other businessmen there whom they convinced to get involved in building a school in one of the Darfur cities in order to make sure that the youth there are being educated.

Raising Money for Gülen-Inspired Projects

A major, if not *the* major focus of Gülen's vision for Turkey and for human-kind, is the importance of quality education for the development of the human person and, simultaneously, for bringing Turkey into the modern era of the twenty-first century. To achieve this goal, he advocated the opening of schools first in Turkey and eventually throughout the world. To do this would require the commitment of everyone in the movement, including administrators, teachers, tutors, students and the financial support of everyone to his/her ability. As a result, every circle in which I interviewed stressed ways in which the circle members support some educational projects, including dormitories, preparatory classes, building schools and providing scholarships for needy students to attend these schools.

Every school has its own independent accounting system and accountants who manage the budget and financial books. They are all accountable to the local and state authorities, as well as to the trust's sponsors. The local sponsors are knowledgeable about the status of the ongoing projects at any given time, for they are personally responsible for many of them, either as construction contractors, accountants, serving on the board of directors, teachers, principals, etc. It is quite easy, therefore, for them to monitor how the donations are used, thereby achieving transparency in financial issues. Moreover, as one businessman explained,

> "First of all, I want you to know that people in the Gülen movement have gained the trust of people in every strata of life. People who support the activities of this movement do not worry about whether the support reached its destination, they don't chase it. However, if we want to look at it, all kinds of information is available in every activity, we can be sure by looking at them."

Likewise, a local businessmen in Houston who finances Gülen-related projects commented, "Even if I don't know the details of their activities, I know these people very well and I trust them. Therefore I make donations knowing they are well used."

In Mardin, for example, a city in southeastern Turkey, a circle of local business-men met over a three year period (1988–1991) and came to realize that the state was unable to provide the necessary education for students not only in their city but throughout southeastern Turkey to compete on university entrance exams. Most of the businessmen had been attending Mr. Gülen's public sermons, in which he emphasized the importance of education and called for the building of modern schools. These businessmen were inspired by the success of the Gülen schools in Izmir, Istanbul and Gaziantep in distinguishing themselves from their counterparts by their research-based education and unprecedented success in international science competitions. During visits to these schools, the men witnessed that the people who donated to the schools included not only businessmen, but also workers, teachers, and civil servants.

In Mardin, these businessmen reached out to more and more people with whom they shared an educational vision and whose help they solicited in sponsoring the schools. Some pledged money, some promised to seek individuals who would pledge to contribute money, others offered to procure construction materials and equipment as donations from their suppliers, and still others committed an amount of physical work in the construction effort. Currently in the Gülen-movement schools in Mardin, every teacher supports the monthly expenses of at least one secondary or high school student.[6]

In a focused interview with a dozen businessmen involved in the small textile industry in Ankara we heard many stories about how the businessmen first became involved with Gülen-inspired projects. For example, in 1985 an imam came to a local mosque and asked the businessmen there for help to open a school for children in the city. After he left, the men gathered together twice each week to discuss the matter. The group made a commitment to assist with the building of the school. Some gave money, others solicited pledges of financial support from other businessmen in the city and others provided goods and services such as concrete, desks, and even volunteer labor. Within a short time, Samanyolu College opened its doors to the first high school class.

The group of businessmen continued to meet routinely, to monitor the needs in the school and to initiate additional projects that they supported. For example, in 1991 after the collapse of the Soviet Union, there was a massacre in Azerbaijan. People there needed help. The Gülen community in Ankara responded; 18 businessmen from different parts of Ankara went to Azerbaijan to deliver money and goods that they had gathered from Gülen-inspired people in Ankara. As one of the businessmen said, "That was an important trip for me. I learned a lot from those people in our group. They were very different people, most of them were not educated like me, but they all affected me in their understanding of Mr. Gülen's teachings and in their lifestyles. Since that trip I am very involved in the Gülen movement."

Another businessman in the focus group told a story that typifies the way in which many people get involved in the movement. One day in 1988 he met a law student who was being financed by one of the businessmen that he knew in his living complex. He asked the businessmen to introduce him to some of these under-privileged law students who could not afford law school. Several days later a group of law students showed up at his store. However, they did not ask for money but talked about country and world problems. A few weeks later they invited the man to their house where there were ten law students gathered from all over Turkey, most of them from poor families. Still there was no talk of money. Some of the students again visited his store and met his son who was having difficulty in school. They offered to tutor the son whose grades improved dramatically with tutoring. There was still no talk of money. The man, after a year of knowing these students

---

[6] Kalyoncu (2008).

personally, initiated scholarships to help them complete law school. He continues since 1988 to provide such scholarships to needy law students.

The above story typifies actions of Mr. Gülen himself in the 1970s and 1980s when he lived on or near university campuses throughout Turkey. He served as a teacher for a time and spent many years supervising students in high school and university settings. In Bursa I interviewed a gentleman who, along with his brother, shared a house with Mr. Gülen while he was attending university in the 1960s. He recalled the many university students who would visit Mr. Gülen in his second story apartment for tutoring and encouragement. He commented that, in his opinion, this cadre of university students who gathered around Mr. Gülen was the beginnings of the Gülen movement in Turkey.

Financial Contributions

Financial giving is an inherent characteristic of participants in the Gülen movement. Repeatedly, interviewees commented that everyone involved in the movement makes some kind of financial contribution depending on his/her circumstances. There was widespread agreement among people in the various local circles that the amount of donations vary between 5% and 20% with 10% of yearly income as an average and a small group of individuals who make contributions above 20%.

Organizational theorists argue that the success of a movement is highly dependent on contributions of "resourceful actors" or elites. Whether they are influential politicians, prophets, successful businessmen, or business firms, these individuals are "resourceful actors" because they have the capacity to contribute a significant part of what it takes to bring about the goals of the movement. The mobilization of a large group happens only when it is facilitated by contributions from such powerful elites because they provide two types of resources: first, elites have access to and often control large resource pools; and, secondly, elite involvement can confer legitimacy and visibility to a social movement, a second resource essential to the success of a movement.[7]

The wealthy industrialists whom I interviewed in Istanbul, including the owner of a major electronics company, the owner of a well established furniture business, and a man whose family owns a shipping company each give about $1 million a year to Gülen-inspired projects, a sum that represents 10–15% of their income. Two of the men are among the five supporters who financed the latest Gülen-inspired hospital in Istanbul. In Bursa, a businessman gives approximately $3.5 million per year which is one third of his income. Another businessman gives $3–4 million per

---

[7] Fireman and Gamson (1979); Olson (1965); McCarthy and Zald (1977); Garner (1996); Melucci (1999); Della Porta and Diani (1999); Morris and Staggenborg (2004).

year to eleven schools in Albania. A third man gives money to schools in ten countries and said he now has brothers in all these countries and not just locally in Turkey.

We asked the group of a dozen businessmen in Ankara whether each of them contributes financially to Gülen-inspired projects and, if so, approximately how much they give each year. Each of the 12 men said that they contribute as they can to the movement projects. Amounts of contributions varied from 10–70% of their annual income, ranging from $20,000 to 300,000 per year. One man, in particular, said he gives 40% of his income every year which is about $100,000; however, he said he would like to give 95% but is not able to do so and still maintain himself and his family. Another man said, "We wish we could be like the companion of the Prophet and give everything we have. But it is not easy." This group of businessmen consisted of older men who have been together as a group for many years and have accomplished numerous Gülen-inspired projects in Ankara as well as in other countries. Currently, each of them has managers in their stores who carry on the daily business affairs. The business owners spend 2–3 hour in their stores every day and then come together almost every day to discuss issues related to the projects they are supporting. The group, therefore, provides a tight community of like-minded individuals working for common causes. Cetin maintains that "the solidarity of the group is inseparable from the personal quest and from the everyday affective and communicative needs of the participants in the network... Yet, it is epiphenomenal, not the ultimate aim or end in itself, by itself, but it accompanies action naturally as a result of the accomplishment of the service projects."[8]

Another very successful businessman in Istanbul whom we interviewed provided insight into the sums of money being contributed by the supporters of the Gülen movement to local projects. He is 48 years old and is in the textile business. He contributes 20% of his $4–5 million yearly income to movement-related projects. Eighty percent of his good friends are also participants in the movement and contribute as they can to projects. He says he has established very sincere and fortunate friendships through participation in activities in the movement. He learned of the movement when a friend in 1986 invited him to a *sohbet* where people come together and have discussions, both about Mr. Gülen's writings and about local projects that need support. Asked what benefits a person gets from supporting Gülen-inspired projects, he replied,

> "I do not get any worldly benefit by supporting the Gülen Movement. If I receive anything in the hereafter, we will see that over there. I hope that I will be able to please God through these activities and the time that I spend with these beautiful people. Other than this, neither I nor other volunteers have any other expectations. After giving your heart to these charitable activities, God never leaves you in trouble. We give and He gives more back to us. He multiplies what we have in our hands. I don't think my contributions are big enough, however, in the sight of God, there is nothing small and valueless if you do that for Him and for humanity."

---

[8] Cetin (2010).

Some of the businessmen and professionals donate one third of their annual income, after taxes, to movement projects. For example, a businessman in Istanbul allocates one third back into his business, one third for the support of his family and the remaining one third to Gülen-related projects. While I was unable to ascertain his yearly income, his business is worth over $1 billion and is among the most successful business enterprises in his economic sector in Turkey. I can surmise, therefore, that his yearly income amounts to multi-millions of dollars. Several people in the movement identify him as one of the largest contributors to the service projects, especially the schools.

The substantial contributions made by wealthy businessmen and entrepreneurs in the movement are important not only for their financial consequences in terms of what can be accomplished in terms of building and sustaining expensive projects but also because such support gives legitimization and visibility to the movement. Throughout interviews frequent mention is made of the "businessmen" who are able to make possible the service goals of the movement.

It is not only the wealthy business owners, however, who contribute financially to the movement but every local circle contributes as it is able to the support of educational projects. The group of young entrepreneurs in Istanbul, many of them engineers, belong to a professional organization of about 1,000 members, all of them participants in the Gülen movement. The group donates about $2 million a year to Gülen-inspired projects. About half of that comes from members themselves and the other half from monies that are solicited by members from family and business associates.

The 10% average for giving within the local circles applies not only to the businessmen and professionals but also to blue collar workers, in Istanbul, Bursa and in Mudanya. Many of these Gülen-inspired participants work as salespersons, bookkeepers, city employees, maintenance workers and employees of factories. The average annual salaries of these workers varied but it is common to make $15,000–30,000 per year. Yet, there was general agreement that the average donation for members in the circle was 10% for most years. If an individual cannot make a 10% monetary contribution, he pledges to solicit contributions from his acquaintances to make up the difference. One worker in Bursa related the incident of arranging for his boss, who knew nothing of the Gülen movement, to visit Albania to see a Gülen-inspired school there. He was so impressed that he now makes a significant financial contribution to the movement every year. Many of the people who are asked to contribute to specific projects are not members of the movement who are already giving. Rather, they are family, friends and acquaintances outside the movement who are willing to financially support needy students or worthwhile service projects, especially during the month of Ramadan when every practicing Muslim is expected to give to charitable giving.

The workers' circles tended to support scholarships rather than schools since the latter is a "bigger item" in terms of financial resources. It usually costs about $1,800 per year to stay in one of the Gülen movement dormitories and workers feel they can afford that type scholarship, either alone or with another circle member.

The workers also help members among themselves who are in need. There are also dormitories in their neighborhoods and members in the circles often know of needy students in these dorms. Also, students visit members and let them know who needs help. Often the children of circle members can stay in local dormitories free of charge and such living arrangement is often favored because it is more conducive for study and for meeting the kinds of friends their parents prefer.

An interesting practice within all of the local circles in which we interviewed is that of publicly announcing one's yearly pledge to Gülen-inspired projects. While great emphasis was placed on the fact that contributions are entirely voluntary and that respect is shown to individual circumstances, interviewees acknowledged that there is competition among circle members regarding how much one can donate. This was especially obvious among the wealthier donors who often challenged one another to increase their pledges. Along with competition, however, several of the participants stated that hearing that one's colleague who makes approximately the same income is pledging to donate a given amount is motivation to do the same. One engineer said, "There is some competition. We know generally what everyone makes and we can compare. When I see that he is giving 10%, it encourages me to do the same."

There are about 50 local interfaith dialog groups in the United States that consist of individuals who are inspired by the teachings and life of Mr. Gülen.[9] These groups are independent organizationally even though members across groups may know another and share ideas and projects informally. The Institute of Interfaith Dialog for World Peace, Inc. (IID) was established in August 2002 in Austin, Texas. One year later the headquarters moved to Houston. IID organizes activities in more than 16 cities in the southern states, including Texas, Louisiana, Oklahoma, Kansas, Arkansas and Mississippi. The purpose of the nonprofit institute, as well as others across the United States, is to promote interfaith dialogue and understanding.

To achieve this purpose, the institute organizes and supports numerous activities in each of the cities in which it has members. These include an annual Ramadan interfaith dinner, a yearly award dinner to honor people in the local communities who make major contributions to interfaith dialog, workshops throughout the year, an annual retreat and numerous interfaith trips to Turkey. These activities are supported financially by contributions on the part of volunteers committed to the institute, most of them Turkish Muslims who are inspired by the teachings of Mr. Gülen. Many of them are Turkish students attending universities in the southern United States, even though there are a handful of businessmen and professionals who are also involved.

Based on the Turkish model of local circles that support Gülen-inspired projects, a large percentage of IID's budget is provided by relatively small contributions on the part of over 500 Turkish and Turkish-Americans in the southern states of the

---

[9] Michels (2008).

U.S. who support projects of IID. About half of these supporters are local students. In the first several years of IID, its annual budget was under $25,000. By 2006 it increased to $500,000 and in 2008 IID collects almost $1 million per year in donations. About 80% comes from the local American Turkish community and the remaining 20% from the non-Muslim local community.

Numerous graduate students, many of them on small stipends from Turkey or from their American universities, pledge $2,000–5,000 every year even though such pledges means great sacrifice on the students' part. It is not unusual for a student on a $1,500 per month stipend to give $100–150 per month to IID which amounts to roughly 10% of his/her income. Some of the students also work in second jobs in order to contribute some money to the activities of IID. And many of them look forward to graduating, having good jobs and being able to contribute more of their income at that point. As one student said, "Being a graduate student it is hard to donate big amounts, but hopefully after I graduate, I will be able to make bigger and better donations."

Approximately 50% of IID members are professionals and businessmen in the community, many of whom have completed education in the United States and have opted to work there for the time being. It is the contributions of these individuals which constitute the largest proportion of IID's income. One local businessman, for example, who is an engineer and has some real estate investments, gives $50,000–70,000 every year to IID which is 40% of his income. He single-handedly finances an Iftar dinner each year. In 2006 he also paid for the tickets for 12 Americans to visit Turkey in an interfaith trip sponsored by IID. He regrets that his busy schedule prohibits him from greater involvement with IID activities; however, he feels he can make an impact in IID projects by providing substantial financial support. In addition, he joins friends every week at *sohbet* (group meetings) to discuss the ideas of Mr. Gülen and how to operationalize them in local projects.

While emphasis has been placed in the organizational literature on the importance of money and legitimacy as resources for successful action, some theorists maintain that volunteer labor has not received equal attention. Much of the impetus for action as well as the day to day activities that propel a movement toward its goals depend on the labor of movement members. Decentralization of authority and a structure whereby tasks are undertaken by committees of volunteers enhances the vibrancy of a movement.[10] This fact is evident in IID as well as in other local Gülen groups. Direct financial contributions do not capture the full picture of donations to Gülen projects. Participants donate time, talents and food to the various activities sponsored by IID. For example, dinner and luncheons are frequently organized by IID. Women in the organization are continuously asked to prepare Turkish food for these gatherings, both small and large, and neither the cost of the food nor the labor involved in preparing it is financially compensated. The design and maintenance of websites, designing fliers and brochures, creating videos related to the activities of IID, organizing events, leading interfaith trips to Turkey, hosting people from other

---

[10]McCarthy and Wolfson (1996); Morris and Staggenborg (2004); Byrne (1997).

faith communities into their homes during Ramadan and networking in the inter-faith community are done by volunteers of the movement. It is not unusual for many IID members to spend 20–30 hours a week in Gülen movement activities, and many of these movement participants are full time students in local universities. If these activities were outsourced or calculated in terms of costs, the donations from IID members would be very substantial.

Some social movement theorists argue that a formalized structure with a clear division of labor leads to a more successful movement and that a centralized decision-making structure increases task effectiveness and the mobilization of resources.[11] However, other research shows that bureaucratic arrangements are less effective at mobilizing grassroots participation and that decentralized structures are more successful in motivating and involving member participation.[12] In the case of the Gülen movement, the decentralized authority and administrative structure promotes member involvement and a sense of responsibility on the part of the millions of participants who maintain a personal stake in the movement achievements.

Motivation Driving the Financial Contributions

When asked why they give $1 million or more dollars each year to movement projects, the group of businessmen in Istanbul gave the following reasons: to make better human beings as Mr. Gülen encourages; to educate our youth; to please God; to earn a reward in the next life; to be part of a bigger movement to better the world; to provide hope to our people in Turkey and around the world. Two of the businessmen were among the first members in the movement who had heard Mr. Gülen preaching in the 1970s and were very impressed with his ideas and came together with other local businessmen to see what they could do to carry out his vision.

The president of a large textile manufacturing company said he is motivated by Mr. Gülen's ideas of service.

> "We get associated with the movement people and this motivates us to get involved with the projects. What are my favorite projects? What is dear to my heart is that I can see these students who graduate and pick up posts in government and become righteous people in government and other offices. When I see these former students in these positions, I am so glad. I see that my society and government is improving in terms of righteousness and free of corruption."

A wealthy businessmen in Istanbul who is a major contributor relayed a story of the first fund raising meeting to build the very first Gülen-inspired school, an event at which Mr. Gülen gave a motivational speech. He said it was important to help needy students and then gave historical examples from the life of the Prophet and

---

[11] Gamson (1975); McCarthy and Zald (1977); McCarthy and Wolfson (1996); Melucci (1999); Morris and Staggenborg (2004).

[12] Gerlach and Hines (1970); Curtis and Zurcher (1974); Jenkins (1983); Byrne (1997).

his companions. At that event I saw people writing checks, giving cash and some offering gold rings and bracelets. "I was deeply impacted by that scene that I saw, giving so immediately and generously. From this first impact, I thought this is something I wanted to be part of. I then saw the successes of the projects and I became part of the movement." He went on to elaborate on other examples of giving that influenced him. He saw blue collar workers with families who were making very little every month but dedicating 20% of their income to support, perhaps, half or one-fourth of a scholarship for a needy student. He realized that these people might be taking public transportation but giving to help students. Later he got involved in fund raising meetings and saw what people were doing to raise money for Gülen-inspired projects, some donating keys to their cars, giving their gold watches and women offering their jewelry to support students. A person in Izmir baked pizzas and sold them from a cart to raise money to build a small dorm in a neighboring small town. The more he witnessed these examples of giving, the stronger was his motivation to do his part to support the worthwhile projects. He made a commitment to donate one third of his income to furthering his business, one third to supporting his family and the remaining one third to Gülen projects.

An engineer, when asked why he gives 10% of his yearly income to the movement, said, "There is no reason other than the pleasure of God. The opposite is it is just working for yourself, greed." And we in the Gülen movement, he continued, are devoted to the spirit of service to humanity which Mr. Gülen taught us.

The blue collar workers were inspired by the fact that Mr. Gülen seemed authentic and, as one worker said, " I was impressed when I heard him that he did not preach one thing that he did not practice himself." Another worker said that he saw fighting and blame on the part of other groups in society but with Gülen he saw love and positive things. He also liked the fact that Mr. Gülen did not have a beard like most imams and taught that Turkey and the Islamic countries must embrace modernity, science and globalization. Another worker expressed the fact the he wanted to get educated but did not have the opportunity. He feels he is now doing something to help someone else be educated.

In several of the local circles, I heard people express the fact that whatever God has given is meant to be shared and that God wants people to be vehicles for the sharing. As one worker said, "We have seen others in the past who are altruistic and share with others as God's vehicle,- so we only feel humble of what we can do."

There is a Turkish tradition that promotes the separation of the donor from the recipient so that a sense of obligation is not created in the one being helped. Also, the giver is seen as a transfer agent from God rather than as a beneficent provider. A businessmen in Bursa who donated land for a school building did not send his own children to the school so that he would not mix personal motivation with doing good works. Another person commented, "We do not want too many details about what we are supporting such as which students get scholarships because it gets too personal. Rather, we donate to a pool that helps needy students but nobody knows who is supporting which ones." However, some of us are in touch with the students receiving help so we know in general how our money is being used.

The 48 year old businessman in Istanbul had this to say," People in the Gülen movement turn their ideas into projects, they tell how they accomplished their success. People trust them, if they ask for a project, they expect it from the Creator, not from creatures, and that's why I believe they reach success. If anybody from the movement comes to my city and asks for help, I try my best to help them and I encourage my friends around me to do the same." He went on to say that such giving is done in a spirit of serving the Creator by serving his people and that often a result of such giving is that strong ties are developed among the givers. As Cetin maintains,

> "Participation in services takes relatively permanent forms of networks. Individuals come and go and replace one another but the projects are always there and continue. Individual needs and collective goals are not mutually exclusive; they are one and the same thing. These two and the action of the Gülen Movement coincide and interweave closely with one another in daily life...The participation in services around a specific goal and the tangibility of the products yield and strengthen solidarity."[13]

An engineer said that people make an investment in their lives with their money and then get a reward in the afterlife if it is invested well. Students, he feels, make a big investment for their lives and he wants to help them make that investment so that they can live productive lives, earn eternal rewards and help others to make that investment once they are educated.

While personal monetary success is not an overt motivation for giving, a number of interviewees at all socio-economic levels commented that often giving to worthwhile projects brings material rewards to the giver: businesses make even greater profits and workers see salary increases or job advancements. These successes are seen as God's blessings on those who give. As one worker said, "When someone gives they see abundance in their incomes; God gives them abundance."

Confidence and Trust in Gülen-Inspired Projects

In every local circle in which I interviewed, members expressed their trust in how their donations were being used. Repeatedly, interviewees said they never worried how their money was being used because they know it is being well spent. Another frequent comment was, "We see results." By this they meant that they see students who are performing well academically in the schools and prep courses. They see students from the Gülen-inspired schools who are accepted into top rated universities in Turkey and abroad. Many of them become members of the movement, often when they are in university. It is also common for some people in the local circles to travel to Central Asian and other countries that have Gülen-inspired schools and to see the contributions these schools are making. Supporters also hear stories about patients who are treated in Gülen-inspired hospitals and are very pleased with their

---

[13] Cetin (2010).

humane treatment by the doctors and staff. The narratives of the many needy people being helped by Kimse Yok Mu, the relief association, are repeated in the local circles and reinforced in the media. Since the Gülen-inspired communities maintain a higher degree of communication through *sohbet* circles and the media, the success stories of Gülen-inspired projects are told and retold, thus assuring contributors that their monies are being well spent and providing tangible results.

Recruitment into the Movement

Many participants in the movement first heard of it when they stayed in the dormitories, attended university with people in the movement or went to one of the preparatory courses. Others heard of it through family or friends. For example, a businessman in Istanbul had a brother in medical school who invited him to Ankara when he was in high school. He stayed with 20 medical school students in one of the Gülen-related dorms. He said immediately he could tell these students were different from other university students in terms of their values, aspirations and attitudes toward one another. He gave the example of sleeping late the first morning and one of the students stayed to make him a big breakfast before going off to study. He was influenced by the group and wanted to know what inspired them to live together in the dorm. He learned that many of them had scholarships to stay there financed by local businessmen. When I became a businessman, I remembered my experience and wanted to be part of the movement by becoming a sponsor for needy students.

Like many of those I interviewed, an engineer first heard about the Gülen movement in university. He was reflecting on his life and trying to find meaning. His cousin introduced him to Gülen-inspired people who were students at the university and living together in a dorm. He joined them and became part of their community.

Other engineers in the group, as well as a number of the doctors I interviewed, first became acquainted with the Gülen movement when attending prep courses in various cities throughout Turkey. One engineer, for example, was looking for intellectual company in his life and did not find it in the far right nationalist group to which he belonged. He said, "When I found Gülen-inspired people at the prep course, I found everything I was looking for. I found religion, nationalism, science, intellectualism and a world view that I could support." He then heard Mr. Gülen speak. He was calling everyone not to fight but to understand one another. He said we are all human beings, on the same ship. As a nationalist, he said, everyone becomes your enemy. When you hear Mr. Gülen, you see that all are really brothers, on the same wave-length. He showed us how Christians, Jews and Muslims all come from the same roots. "Mr. Gülen opened our eyes to see we are friends with other people. Before we saw them as different from us, he taught us to see them as close to us." He went on to say that we can help one another, even in our careers and businesses, and that we need to think globally and support our friends to even go abroad rather than just focusing on Turkey.

A factory worker enrolled in a state sponsored prep course in Istanbul but saw that the students who completed the course were not very successful in scoring high enough to enter university. He met some students who were enrolled in a Gülen-inspired prep course who were much more serious about studying and getting an education so he transferred into that course. There he came to know and respect members of the Gülen movement, especially the teachers in the course who were very dedicated and spent time with the students beyond the required classroom teaching. He wanted to know what motivated them and began to talk with them about Mr. Gülen and his ideas. He was very impressed and wanted to be like them.

Generating Commitment

A major empirical finding of Kanter's study of American utopias that has subsequently influenced the commitment literature is that for a community to survive, three basic challenges of commitment have to be addressed.[14] First, individuals come to see their own interest as sustained by group participation.[15] Secondly, individuals feel an affective solidarity with the group,[16] and, thirdly, the individual experiences a moral, transcendent authority in the group.[17] These mechanisms can be summarized as strategies by which the group attempts to reduce the value of other possible commitments and increases the value of commitment to the group; in other words, processes both detaching him or her from other options and attaching him to the community. In particular, Kanter's research shows a positive correlation between sacrifice and investment in terms of generating commitment. The more costly the sacrifice, the greater the value placed by the individual on the goals of the group. Data in this book support Kanter's contention by showing that financial contributions to Gülen-inspired projects not only manifest belief in the goals of the movement but that the giving itself is a commitment mechanism for involvement in the group.

In Kanter's conceptualization, the goals of the group become fused with one's own sense of purpose and meaning in life. Group goals nourish one's own sense of self and the group becomes an extension of oneself, thus inextricably linking person and group, thus meeting the first of Kanter's basic challenges for group survival and success. Interviews with supporters in the Gülen movement demonstrate that they identify the goals of the movement as their own personal goals. Being part of the Gülen movement, participating in the local circles, and making contributions to the projects supported by the movement is central to their identity.

---

[14] Kanter (1968).

[15] Konovsky and Pugh (1994); Rioux and Penner (2001).

[16] Van Vugt and De Cremer (1999); Fine (1986); Jacobsen (1988).

[17] Hales (1993).

The affective bonds that evolve in the group in the course of working together on meaningful projects fulfills Kanter's second organizational challenge. The fact that many local circles are based on individuals who share occupational or business interests further adds to the solidarity created in the group. The more closely an individual is integrated into a group, the greater will be the degree of his/her participation.[18] Participation is an expression of belonging to a certain social group and receiving individual rewards for being part of the larger collective. Also, the more intense the collective participation in a network of relations, the more rapid and durable will be the mobilization of a movement.[19] The Gülen Movement facilitates and thus increases an individual's willingness to get involved in service projects through his/her relationship with other like-minded, similarly intentioned people.

The third challenge, the experience of a moral, transcendent authority in the group is provided by the continuous discussions of Mr. Gülen's teachings as well as sharing readings from the Qur'an and the hadiths of the Prophet. Thus, the goals and motivations behind the service projects are more than just helping other people. Rather, they are rooted in the notion that they are part of God's continuous creation and caring for his people.

Kanter argues that a further mechanism for individual commitment to group life and group goals is that of sacrifice. The giving of one's time and resources to the group not only indicates commitment to the group but also creates that very commitment. As people in the Gülen movement give of their personal resources to group life and group projects, the very act of giving has the consequence of intensifying commitment to the group and its ideals.

The basic Islamic ideals that motivate members of the Gülen movement to contribute time, energy and financial contributions to Gülen-inspired projects function, simultaneously, to build strong commitment on the part of individuals to the movement. A major strength of the local circles is the constant discussions of these concepts based on the Qur'an, the prophetic tradition and the works of Mr. Gülen. The circles, therefore, provide the spiritual motivation for giving and remain far more than simply money raising venues. Whether consciously or not, the structure that has evolved within the Gülen movement is rooted in sound organizational principles and is reflected in the growth of the movement worldwide.

---

[18] Klandermans (1989).

[19] Melucci (1999).

The Turkish–Islamic Culture of Giving*

In order to understand the impetus and motivation behind the service commitment and financial support on the part of millions of Turkish people for the Gülen movement, it is necessary to understand certain cultural-religious practices related to philanthropy and charity in Turkish history. It is clear that the movement started in Turkey and that its activities are organized predominantly by Turkish citizens and by Turks in the diaspora around the world. Numerous scholars have concluded, for better or for worse, that the movement is inherently tied to Turkish culture and a specifically Turkish understanding of Islam.[1] Other scholars have aptly described it as a movement "witnessing [to] tradition in the modern age," and that it is Turkish Islam that is at the heart of the tradition.[2] It is impossible, therefore, to analyze what motivates Turkish people to give so generously to the activities of the movement without understanding concepts of giving and hospitality that are inherent in Turkish culture.

One of the aspects of the Gülen movement that has been discussed in recent media without sufficient attention to the cultural-historical context has been the issue of how the movement finances its plethora of institutions and activities. In addition to some limited scholarly investigations of this issue,[3] some Turkish and international newspapers, magazines, television stations and blog spots have printed and/or broadcast a number of accusations about the movement's financial sources. Underlying allegations that the movement has received aid from such contradictory foreign sources as the CIA, Mossad, the Vatican, Saudi Arabia, Iran, and the Russian Federation, are political and ideological opponents' presumptions that the many individuals who support the movement's institutions and activities, both financially and through volunteering or official association, are motivated by intent

---

* Co-authored with Dr. Zachary Baskal

[1] Yavuz and Esposito (2003); Park (2007); Fuller (2008).

[2] Ozdalga (2000); Michel (2005); Ergene (2007).

[3] Ebaugh and Koç (2007); Kalyoncu (2008).

to gain political power and/or convert the nation/world to radical Islam or Catholicism. However, our interview data show that almost all supporters of the movement, be they Turkish-Muslim participants or non-Turkish, non-Muslim sympathizers, are motivated by a genuine philanthropic urge to give. Graham Fuller, former vice chairman of the National Intelligence Council at the CIA, political scientist for the RAND Corporation, and expert on both the Middle East and the Muslim world, explains, for example, that the number of Gülen-inspired schools is ever expanding thanks to the generosity of wealthy businessmen who see such work not only as a form of *zekat* (alms-giving as a means of assisting the less fortunate and reducing economic inequality), but also as the realization of *ihsan*, the deeper spiritual motivation to put one's faith in action for the purpose of perfecting spiritual excellence by "doing beautiful things." He says further that:

> ...the Gülen movement has launched a flag-ship program that has built a network of hundreds of schools. Funding comes from within the community and from wealthy businessmen for whom building a school has become the modern pious equivalent of building a mosque.[4]

Fuller's explanation of why Turkish-Muslim businessmen are so eager to fund the movement's educational initiatives relies on specifically Islamic concepts. Hence, a brief exploration of the culture of giving and hospitality in Turkey, in particular, and in Islam in general, will shed light on issues related to the Gülen movement's activities, its financial sources, and the motivations of the many people who contribute to the movement in various ways. The most important element in any altruistic social movement, including the Gülen movement, is the desire of its members to give of their time, money, and energy without expecting a material gain in return. In this chapter, we demonstrate that some of the key elements that define and determine the characteristics of the Gülen movement, such as belief in and practice of virtues like self-sacrifice, charity and philanthropy, are deeply rooted in Turkish–Islamic culture.

The values of giving and showing hospitality have deep historical roots in Turkish culture. Traditions related to generosity, hospitality and charity can be traced back to the central Asian civilizations from which Turks hail. Nomadic Turks living in central Asia accepted Islam in the ninth and tenth centuries. Among the various reasons for these Turks' ready acceptance of Islam is the existence of many similarities between their pre-Islamic lifestyles, values and ethics and those that Islam prescribes. Most certainly, Islam strengthened, institutionalized and added a spiritual dimension to pre-Islamic Turkish culture in addition to discontinuing some undesirable practices – just as occurred in other major religions' interaction with local cultures.

Some habits, practices and traditions which are usually attributed to Islam might very well have been inherited from pre-Islamic Turkish culture. However, since Islam introduced very similar customs and traditions, it is difficult to tell which ones

---

[4]Fuller (2008).

come from Islam and which ones come from Turkish culture. Considering the high likelihood that most Islamic and pre-Islamic Turkish traditions related to giving and hospitality overlap, we will treat them as an inherent part of "Turkish culture" for the rest of the chapter. We should also point out the fact that the worldviews and practices of certain religious orders (for example, the Mawlawīyah Sufi Order of Konya) and their cultural-religious products (for example, Mawlānā Jalāl ad-Dīn Muhammad Rūmī's six-volume poem, the *Mathnawīye Ma'nawī*) have both crys-tallized and become identical with the cultural norms of the region in such a way that is impossible to distinguish one from the other.

One of the most important sources of early Turkish history is a text called the *Dede Korkut* stories, accounts which are set in the heroic age of Oghuz Turks in the eighth century A.D. These epic legends document the transition of Turkish clans from a shamanist to a Muslim society, as well as the continuance of a distinguished culture of hospitality and giving. For example, along with accounts of Oghuz Turks drinking alcohol and eating horse meat, which are not common habits among Muslims today, we find a narrator's description of a man performing the call to prayer (*ezan*) – "when the long-bearded Persian recites the call to prayer," an act which strongly indicates that the new religion was not yet completely accepted as an inherent element of Turkish society. These same stories also elaborately describe social gatherings and invitations to gatherings, at which either the head of the clan or the head of the household organizes a great feast and distributes plentiful gifts to the guests. Indeed, pre-Islamic Turks designated numerous occasions for feast-giving, such as births, weddings, name-giving ceremonies, clan members' return from a foreign land, wish-making rituals, and deaths. Among the ancient Turkish practices still alive in contemporary Turkey are wedding feasts, family visits to request a girl's hand in marriage, and the slaying of an animal (i.e. a feast) for guests.

Today Turkish society is known for its **hospitality (*misafirperverlik*).** Routinely, people who visit the country attest to the warmth of Turkish hospitality. The author of *Tradition and Change in a Turkish Town* explains this phenomenon as follows:

> The importance of hospitality and generosity among Turks and other Middle Easterners is difficult to exaggerate. Any Middle Easterner who enjoys a reputation for these two virtues is respected and admired by members of his community. Guests in a Turkish home must be treated like royalty. They are offered the best places; food and drink, everyone in the household turns his full attention to their comfort. [...]In return, guests must be extremely polite and grateful. One of the most appreciated forms of thanks they can offer is the phrase: "May Allah accept you[r efforts]," denoting that generosity and hospitality are pious virtues.[5]

In numerous anthropological works, Turkish hospitality is taken for granted, and interestingly, little attention has been paid to the reasons behind society members' overwhelmingly positive attitude toward guests and the duties of hospitality.[6]

---

[5] Magnarella (1974).

[6] See, for example, Piece (1964), Magnarella (1974), and Delaney (1991). These authors are appre-ciative of Turkish hospitality, but they provide little explanation for it.

Although the forms of Turkish hospitality are changing in industrialized and urbanized areas, due to changing work habits and demographics, hospitality is still easily observed. The many expressions and beliefs maintaining and encouraging the culture of hospitality in contemporary Turkey have their roots in Islam, but also in pre-Islamic nomadic culture.

The *Dede Korkut* stories, for example, provide many examples of Turkish hospitality. When a clan member dies, relatives slaughter his horses and give a funeral feast. When the leaders in society are about to make a decision or announcement that will affect everyone, they invite their tribes' members to a lavish feast and let them loot the table, including the plates. Some stories contain references condemning or at least belittling the houses or tents that do not receive guests. Dede Korkut, the sage and holy man of clan society at that time, states: "The black tents to which no guest comes would be better destroyed." In these stories, it is believed that if one feeds the poor, pleases guests, or gives a big feast, one's wishes will come true. The following is the advice of a wife whose husband wants a child, but has not been able to sire one for many years:

Rise and bestir yourself, have the tents of many colors
Set up on the earth's face. Have your man slaughter
Of horses the stallions, of camels the males, of sheep the rams.
Gather round you the nobles of Inner Oghuz and Outer Oghuz
When you see the hungry, fill him;
When you see the naked, clothe him;
Save the debtor from his debt.
Heap up meat in hillocks; let lakes of kumis be drawn
Make an enormous feast, and ask what you want and let them pray
So, with prayerful mouths singing your praises,
God may grant us a fine hefty child.[7]

Other expressions and practices of hospitality might also be remnants of pre-Islamic culture, even though Islam supports a similar approach. For instance, if a stranger knocks at the door, s/he should be invited inside, given ample food and shelter for three days; and only at the end of three days should the cause of the visit be asked. This time frame of three days is specified both by oral Turkish folklore, common proverbs,[8] and by various oral traditions

---

[7]Dede Korkut (1974).

[8]See, for example, the Turkish proverb, "A guest is a guest for three days," also known as "Guesthood lasts three days." This proverb indicates that a three day stay is acceptable for both parties, and that staying longer may involve a burden on the host, unless the guest begins helping with the household chores like a family member.

about the life, speech and practices (hadiths) of the Prophet Muhammad. Moreover, Turks call a guest who arrives without prior knowledge of the host "a guest from God" (*Tanrı misafiri*).

The peculiar usage of the Turkish word *Tanrı*, rather than Arabic or Persian, indicates the possibility that the name for an unexpected guest hails from the pre-Islamic period. Indeed, when the narrator of *Dede Korkut* classifies women into three categories and describes their respective features, he praises most the type of woman who hosts and feeds the guest, even if her husband is not at home. This practice was later approved by religion – albeit with some restrictions concerning physical divisions of space in the home, and men's and women's clothing, speech and behavior while in mixed company – and has continued to exist as part of Turkish culture to this day.

However, it is also possible that the expression derives from a Qur'anic reference to the Prophet Abraham's hospitable reception of three "unknown" guests, who turned out to be the Archangel Gabriel and two other angels, bringing him the glad tidings of a son to be born to his wife, Sarah, and warning him of the destruction of Sodom and Gomorrah, save for his nephew Lot and a handful of believers. The religious motivation for graciously accepting unexpected guests, travelers, or even strangers at one's door is also expressed in a rhyming proverb, which says that "one has to consider every night a Night of Power, and every arriving person, Khizr." (*"Her geceyi Kadir, her geleni de Hızır bil"*). This proverb makes reference to the personality of Khizr, a Muslim saint or prophet believed to appear in time of need, who has been granted special knowledge of the Unseen, and whose spirit has been known to appear to pious individuals on earth; hence, Turks are encouraged to treat strangers who knock on their doors as well as they would treat a visiting saint. The proverb also suggests that hospitality in everyday life is as important as spiritual readiness for the Night of Power, an unspecified night in the latter half of Ramadan which is considered "more valuable than one thousand months," as expressed in the Qur'an (97:3).

There are other specifically Islamic concepts and practices of giving which quickly took root in ancient Turkish culture, migrated with nomadic Turks across the steppes of central Asia to Anatolia, and later entered northern Africa and the Balkans under the auspices of the Ottoman Empire. Certain acts of giving prescribed by the Qur'an and encouraged by the Prophet Muhammad (570–632 A.D.) have found almost continuous cultural translation in pre-Ottoman, Ottoman and modern Turkish society. The major concepts to be discussed are: **sadaka**, **zekat**, **kurban**, **vakıf**, **ahilik**, **bereket**, **komşuluk** and **karz-i hasen**. In this context, we will also examine the sociolinguistic significance of common Turkish idioms and proverbs related to giving, hospitality and neighborliness. Finally, we will briefly suggest ways in which the ideals, activities and discourse of the Gülen movement have provided a new outlet for individual and group expression of Turkish-Islamic traditions related to giving.

Major Concepts in Turkish Culture Related to Giving

Sadaka

One of the most important prophetic practices that encourages Turks to give is *sadaka,* a term which can be translated as "charity," "alms" or "a charitable gift which is given with the sole intention of pleasing God and in expectation of a reward in the Hereafter (i.e. without calculation of any worldly gain, such as fame, power or societal recognition).[9] The recipients of *sadaka* are not obliged to be members of any particular religion. Anyone who needs charity can receive a donation. Although *sadaka* is usually interpreted as something tangible or monetary, hadiths relate that any favor given, even the act of smiling at a fellow Muslim, can be considered a *sadaka*, with its giver promised a spiritual reward. Hence, people can offer money, food, water, clothes, books, professional expertise or their time as *sadaka*. References to *sadaka* in various hadiths stress, in particular, the excellence of alms given under one or another circumstance: for example, *sadaka* given to close neighbors and relatives, *sadaka* given on Fridays or during Ramadan, *sadaka* given in Makkah, Madinah or Jerusalem, *sadaka* given in secret, and *sadaka* involving self-sacrifice are said to be particularly meritorious.[10]

Giving *sadaka* has remained a widespread practice in modern Turkish culture, whether individuals define themselves as religious or not. In Ottoman times, *sadaka* was given on many occasions and placed anonymously either in the mosque collection box, on a "*sadaka* stone" outside the mosque or in the street, or in the hand of a representative of a *vakıf* (charitable trust) or the local government, both of which ran soup kitchens (*a evleri*) open to the public. These practices assured that individuals in need of charity could easily take what they needed without sacrificing their family honor or personal dignity.[11] Most Ottoman Turks subscribed to the Islamic belief that a *sadaka* given sincerely helps a Muslim to ward off trouble in this world, makes his/her interrogation in the grave easier, and serves to elevate one's status in the Hereafter.[12] Even though the westernization movement, which began in the Tanzimat Period and gained almost irresistible force during the early years of the Turkish Republic, introduced secular and nationalist values into every area of life in a "top down" manner, it can be argued that what was introduced

---

[9]Interestingly, the Arabic word for charity, *sadaqah*, derives from *sidq*, meaning truth.

[10]For more detailed information on the hadiths referencing sadaka, see the "Sadaka" entry in *The Encyclopedia of Islam,* Vol 26.

[11]For more information about the practice of *sadaka* during Ottoman times, see historical lectures by Dr. Talha Uğurluel (televised regularly by Samanyolu TV) or lectures/works by renowned historian Dr. İlber Ortaylı.

[12]These ideas have been explained by scholars like İbrahim Hakkı, whose works have played an important role in helping today's Turks to understand and practice their religion. Ibrahim Hakkı, Ruhul Beyan, Istanbul: 1928.

presented no real alternative to Islam, which had provided Anatolians with identity and organizing principles of life for so long. Richard Tapper[13] says, "At the public level, it was no substitute for the divine laws of Islam; at the individual level, it could not meet the intellectual needs for an ethics and eschatology." Hence, many Islamic practices, like *sadaka*, have survived into the modern period.

In modern Turkish society, *sadaka* is given on many occasions, albeit in perhaps a less consciously religious manner by some individuals. The most common occasions for giving *sadaka* (via the collection box in one's local mosque, the timely sacrifice of a ram or cow (*kurban*) and the distribution of its meat to the poor, or an electronic transfer of funds to a charity organization) are: before a young couple has a baby or after the baby is born; before taking a trip or after completing the trip; before starting a project and after the completion of the project; after having a bad dream and in order to prevent malicious interpretation of the dream; before families marry off their children and after a wedding ceremony; when parents hear the news that their children are expecting a baby and after the baby is born; before they send their sons to do military service and after the son returns from service. More religiously minded Turks might keep a *sadaka* box near the entrance of their home and deposit loose change into it every time they go out. They might also give *sadaka* to atone for a sin or to express thankfulness to God for having been spared from a great disaster. *Sadaka* is given by people who are alive as well as in the name of those who are deceased. A prophetic tradition that will be discussed extensively in the section on *vakıflar* (charitable trusts) encourages the offspring of a deceased person to give *sadaka*. For this reason, children of the deceased often look for an occasion to give *sadaka* in order to please not only God, but also the spirits of their fathers, mothers or loved ones.

Zekat

Although *sadaka* is a voluntary payment or contribution, most Turks recognize a religiously institutionalized and mandatory form of it called **zekat**. *Zekat* is the obligatory payment of a certain portion (1/40th) of one's total wealth – if one possesses more capital or property than what is absolutely necessary to maintain the livelihood of one's family – to the poor once a year. This giving away of lawfully earned wealth to the needy is regarded as bringing about its purification and increase, as charity is likened in the Qur'an to the sowing of seed which brings immense reward:

> The parable of those who spend their wealth in God's cause is like that of a grain that sprouts seven ears, and in every ear, there are a hundred grains. God multiplies for whom He wills. God is All-Embracing (with His Mercy), All-Knowing. (2:261).

---

[13] Tapper (1991).

The Turkish understanding of Islam generally corresponds to the Sunni interpretation of Islam, which stipulates that every Muslim who is able to fulfill the five tenets of Islam. Along with verbally testifying, "I witness that there is no god but God, and Muhammad is his servant and prophet," praying five times a day, fasting, and making the pilgrimage to Mecca, *zekat* is an important tenet for those believers who qualify economically. References in the Qur'an make *zekat* a mandatory act for many Muslims. *Zekat* cannot be considered a voluntary act of giving because it is part of the tenets of Islam; and a person does not have the right not to give if he/she qualifies economically. According to the Qur'an and many hadiths, the recipients of *zekat*, ie. the poor, have a natural and inherent right to it; and in giving *zekat*, the payer is simply fulfilling his/her religious duty, rather than doing something extra. In Islamic literature, *zekat* is recognized as an important means of redistributing wealth among the members of society, and for the role it plays in preventing certain social ills exacerbated by poverty, such as theft and prostitution. Indeed, regular alms-giving for the benefit of the poor is known to contribute to the harmony and prosperity of societies. *Zekat*, ideally, should cement relationships between various sectors of the community and provide stability. It should cultivate a civic spirit, solve social problems, and foster bonds of love and friendship between members of society.[14] Qur'anic verses which deem *zekat* a mandatory act, threaten those Muslims who are not willing to pay it with Hell-fire.[15]

Two Quranic verses (2:117 and 9:60) provide a detailed list of the sort of people who could be *zekat* recipients: needy relatives and neighbors, orphans, the poor and destitute, those who are burdened by debts, travelers experiencing hardship, slaves or captives in need of emancipation, *zekat* collectors (who were themselves among the needy), and those "whose hearts" are to be "won over" to God's cause. Later, Muslim jurists developed groups or subgroups under these categories and expanded the number of people who could receive charity through *zekat*. As a result, the general rule for giving *zekat* is to start from the center (i.e., with those people closest to oneself) and extend to the periphery. In other words, an obliged Muslim should give *zekat* first to needy relatives and neighbors, and then, only if there are no eligible recipients in these two categories, to other needy people. Also, local distribution of *zekat* is preferred to national or regional distribution.

Another form of mandatory *zekat* or *sadaka* is *sadaka-yı fıtır*, giving that is due at the end of Ramadan each year. *Sadaka-yı fıtır* is usually between $10 and $25, or the amount of money needed to feed a needy person for one day.[16] Unlike *zekat*, which is an obligation for Muslims of a certain age and economic status, *sadaka-yı*

---

[14] Karakaş (2002).

[15] See, for example, this Qur'anic verse: "Let not those who are niggardly with what God has granted them out of His bounty think that it is good for them: rather, it is bad for them. What they are niggardly with, they will have it hung about their necks on the Day of Resurrection. (Why are they niggardly, seeing that to God belongs the absolute ownership of the heavens and the earth?) And He will inherit them in the end. And God is fully aware of all that you do." (3:180).

[16] In the past, sacks of grain, dates or grapes were also considered valid *sadaka-yı fıtır*.

fıtır should be paid by every single member of the family who is economically able. *Sadaka-yı fıtır* is viewed as a means of "evening the scales" to allow poor members of society to celebrate *Eid-ul-Fitr*, a major holiday at the end of the month of Ramadan.

In early Islamic history, *zekat* was collected by the state, in the form of a tax. In later centuries, it seems to have been collected rigorously at times, while at other times individuals paid it if they so chose. Even under such highly bureaucratized administrations as the Ottoman (mid-thirteenth to early twentieth centuries), there does not seem to have been a formal method of wealth assessment for *zekat*, so that the amount paid would have been a matter of personal conscience.[17] In the early twentieth century, as the Islamic caliphate gave way to colonized or semi-colonized nation-states, and many governments gave up collecting *zekat* in favor of western-ized tax systems, the decision of whether or not individual citizens should pay *zekat* was officially left to them. In Turkey, when nationalist/secularist initiatives disas-sembled many Islamic institutions in the 1930s, the Turkish Aeronautical Association (*Türk Hava Kurumu* founded in 1925) was designated as a non-profit organization to which citizens could pay *zekat*. Out of concern that this organiza-tion might not adhere closely to religious stipulations, other budding civic organiza-tions also began to assume the task of collecting and distributing *zekat*. Indeed, in contemporary Turkey, *zekat* has become a very important financial source for non-governmental charity organizations and civil society, in general.

One important component of giving *sadaka*, *zekat* or *sadaka-yı fıtır* is secrecy. Prophetic tradition states that "the left hand should not see what the right hand spends," which means that *sadaka* or *zekat* should be given in total secrecy. Considering the small and close-knit society in which the Prophet Muhammad lived, as well as the nature of many societies' town and village life, the honor and dignity of the people who receive *sadaka* from the very same people with whom they live, work and socialize, this principle becomes very important. A well-known Turkish proverb also reflects the religious motivation to do good deeds in secret: "Do goodness and throw it into the sea. If fish do not appreciate it, for sure the Creator will" (" *yilik yap, denize at; balık bilmese Halık bilir*"). There are, however, cases in which *sadaka* or fundraising for the benefit of the poor has been done openly, and wealthy people have been encouraged to give even more. One famous example in Islamic history is the fundraising done by the Prophet Muhammad in Madinah. When the newly growing Muslim community needed money, Prophet Muhammad asked his companions to go to their homes and bring back some money. Umar ibn Al-Khattab, who would later become the second caliph, brought half of what he had; and Abu Bakr As-Siddiq, who later became the first caliph, brought all of his wealth. When Abu Bakr was asked what he had left for his family, he answered, "I left them God and His Messenger. Even though 'Umar ibn Al-Khattab is said to have then understood that he could never outdo Abu Bakr

---

[17] McChesney (1995).

As-Siddiq in terms of loyalty to the Islamic cause, both men continue to serve as Muslim models of generosity to this day.

Other Turkish–Islamic traditions related to giving and charity practiced during the holy month of Ramadan and the two major holidays, *Eid-ul Fitr* (Ramazan Bayramı) and *Eid-ul Adha* (*Kurban Bayramı*), may also be discussed within the context of *sadaka* and *zekat*. During Ramadan, one of the many ways in which a believer can earn merit in God's sight is to invite guests to one's home for *iftar*, the fast-breaking meal at sunset, or for *sahur*, the early morning meal before the fast begins. In Ottoman times, this custom developed new intricacies, as generous hosts sought to please their guests, not only by feeding them a dizzying array of delicious dishes, but also by offering them small gifts, known as *diş kirası*, in an attempt to win over their hearts and prayers. Beyond the family, Ottoman *vakıflar* (*philanthropic trusts*) and local government agencies held public *iftars* outdoors, ensuring that both the poor and rich alike could break their fasts. Today, the tradition of "fast-breaking tents" (*iftar çadırları*), free and open to the public, has been revived by Turkey's municipal governors, who view such charitable, democratic events as mutually beneficial for the rich and poor. During *Eid-ul Fitr*, also known as "*Ramazan Bayramı*" ("Ramadan Holiday"), even Turks who do not pay *zekat* or *sadaka-yı fıtır* make an effort to give small gifts of candy and money to all the children they know or see while paying visits to relatives, friends and neighbors.

Kurban

During *Eid-ul Adha*, also known as "*Kurban Bayramı*" or "Feast of the Sacrifice," most Turkish Muslims, like Muslims worldwide, offer sacrifices in the form of farm animals such as sheep or cattle, in commemoration of the willingness of the Prophet Abraham to sacrifice his son as an act of obedience to God, and in commemoration of the generosity with which God accepted his sincere intent, instructing him to sacrifice a ram instead (Qur'an 37:102–107). This second major Islamic holiday coincides with the day after the pilgrims conduct hajj, the annual pilgrimage to Mecca. The day is the source of a number of strong cultural traditions related to giving and charity. For example, most Turks who sacrifice an animal act in accordance with the Quran (22:28, 34–37) and Prophetic tradition, dividing the meat into three shares: one share for the poor (i.e. *sadaka*), one share for relatives and neighbors, and the last for themselves. In recognition that a large portion of the meat must be given to poor and hungry people so that they can all join in the feast, many Turks donate all or most of their meat, as well as the animal skins and bones, to civic organizations responsible for distribution. The remainder is cooked for the family celebration meal which relatives and friends are invited to share. The regular charitable practices of Turkish Muslims are demonstrated during *Eid ul-Adha* by the concerted effort to see that no impoverished person is left without sacrificial food, and that no close relatives, especially elderly relatives, and friends are left unvisited during these days.

Turks' inclination to sacrifice a farm animal in the name of God (*bismillah*) and distribute the meat to the poor (i.e. give *sadaka*) after a baby is born and its first tress of hair is cut, is the continuation of a pre-Islamic custom on the Arabian peninsula. This tradition, called *akide*, was approved and institutionalized by the Prophet Muhammad during the early years of Islam. It is also common for Turks to make a *sadaka* of sacrificial meat upon opening a new business or upon any of the occasions listed above, in which monetary *sadaka* is given.

Vakıf

Another important institution that reflects the culture of giving in Turkish culture is the **vakıf** (charitable trust). Charitable trusts had their golden age in Turkish culture during the Ottoman period (1299–1920) and can be called the *par excellence* of giving. The Arabic term *waqf* can be translated as "common law trust" or "endowed free will offering." In order to establish an inalienable religious endowment, an adult who was of sound mind, who was capable of handling financial affairs, who was not under interdiction for bankruptcy, and who intended to perform a pious deed, would declare part or all of his or her property, typically a building or a plot of land, to be a *vakıf*, i.e. devoted to Muslim religious or charitable purposes. Generally, this decision was irrevocable. In order to secure the *vakıf*, the individual who declared it would then go to court and attempt to repossess the property, whereupon the court would issue a statement that the property is a *vakıf* and cannot be returned, sold or donated. Establishment of a *vakıf* also included the formal designation of beneficiaries (i.e. family members, a particular segment of the public, and/or public utilities) and appointment of a trustee or board of trustees (*mutevelli*), who would manage the *vakıf* according to the original purpose and laws by which it was established. These trustees possessed the right to make changes as long as these were in accordance with Islamic law and to the benefit of the foundation; in other cases, permission from a judge had to be sought. Improper management of a *vakıf*, especially improper use of its funds, was regarded as a sin. Although some scholars believe that early Islamic endowments were modeled after those of Christians and Zoroastrians, with whom Arab Muslims came in contact in the seventh century,[18] virtually all Turks ascribe an Islamic origin to the establishment.

Although *waqfs* are not mentioned specifically in the Qur'an, numerous prophetic traditions encourage their establishment. In the Islamic legal view, the institution originated when Umar ibn al-Khattab acquired land in the oasis of Khaybar near Mecca. He asked the Prophet whether he should give the land away as a voluntary donation (*sadaka*) and the Prophet is reported to have replied, "Encumber

---

[18] McChesney (1995).

the thing itself and devote its fruits to pious purposes." Umar reportedly did this
with the provision that the land should neither be sold nor inherited, and he dedicated its income for a variety of charitable purposes – for the manumission of
slaves, for travelers, for guests and "in the way of God."[19] Another famous hadith
recounts: "The Messenger of God said: When a man dies, only three deeds will
survive him: continuing alms, profitable knowledge and a child praying for him."[20]
Whereas the second of these items, "profitable knowledge" was interpreted as production of a book or a successive line of students, the first item, "continuing alms"
was interpreted as the continuance of a charitable trust.

Charitable trusts reached their peak in Ottoman society. Wealthy, pious men and
women designated huge plots of land and whole buildings, as well as smaller plots
of land, single houses and even single rooms as *vakıf*. There were also cases in
which a single carpet or rug was declared a *vakıf* for a particular school or mosque,
or in which libraries or single books were declared as *vakıf* and presented to the
public for common use. Charitable trusts were widespread, not only among
Muslims, but also among Christians and Jews living under Ottoman rule. In large
cities, in government centers, and even in provincial towns, hundreds of charitable
trusts were established for various purposes. Some *vakıfs* addressed the needs of
animals: helping weak birds unable to migrate to warmer lands, hatching chickens
in ovens, taking care of stray cats and dogs, and providing veterinary services.
Other *vakıfs* were dedicated to the needs of individuals or groups of people. As both
people and public utilities could be the beneficiaries of a charitable trust, endowments were established for the construction and maintenance of roads, schools,
mosques, water utilities, public baths, bridges, graveyards and drinking fountains,
as well as for the financial support of students, widows, orphans, and the poor of
designated neighborhoods. Muslims, as well as Christians and Jews, could establish
and take advantage of the benefits of such trusts. Especially in the Balkans, where
the population was predominately Christian in the early years of Ottoman rule,
charitable trusts played an important role in performing civic functions and helping
the weak and needy in the region, thereby securing the admiration and sympathy of
the local population.

In essence, charitable trusts provided many services that modern state and local
governments provide, such as provision of health care and elementary education,
road maintenance, and distribution of clean water to towns and cities. In addition to
serving the poor and needy, *vakıf* also increased public respect for the rich who had
established the endowments. In short, the existence of *vakıf* promoted social harmony and reduced the gap between rich and poor.

The *vakıf* tradition continued vigorously from the twelfth century to the nineteenth century, serving many positive functions in Ottoman society. In 1910, the
Young Turks replaced them with Chambers of Commerce; and in 1920, they were

---

[19] Ibn Had j ar al-Askalānī, Bulūg h al-marām, Cairo n.d., no. 784. In: "WaÐf", *Encyclopedia of Islam (EI-2)*.

[20] ibid., no. 783.

brought under the jurisdiction of the Ministry of Religious Affairs and Charitable Trusts which was then changed to a General Directorship of Charitable Trusts in 1924. The general directorship continues to oversee some 41,000 charitable trusts remaining from Ottoman times and owns one of the largest banks in the country, Vakıf Bank, which employs more than 38,000 people.[21] Today in Turkey, many types of charitable trusts exist. Some provide funds for restoration and preservation of the country's countless historical sites, while others provide financial, educational, cultural and/or health services to the public. Today's *vakıfs* are also complemented by a plethora of charitable organizations and associations whose activities are often similar, even though their financial and legal structures differ.

Comparatively speaking, institutionalized forms of philanthropy, such as the *vakıf*, are easier to trace than informal forms of philanthropy, such as *sadaka*, due to the practices and contributions of *vakıf* institutions, which typically leave a paper trail of legal documents.

Ahi Organizations

In addition to *vakıflar*, **Ahi** organizations are also examples of charitable giving. *Ahi* organizations are social, professional, religious groupings that appeared in Anatolia in the thirteenth century and played an important role in the foundation of the Ottoman Empire. *Ahi* organizations are related to *futuwwa* or *fityan* which are various movements and organizations which, until the beginning of the modern era, were widespread throughout all the urban communities of the Muslim east."[22] They were a form of chivalry with two important elements, their connection with Sufism and their professional dimensions. As a professional grouping, they were linked to Ahi Evran (d.1262) who is considered to be the patron saint of tanners. There were various trade organizations in Turkey but the tanners became the prominent umbrella organization due to their centralized location and firm organizational structure. The representative of Ahi Evran lived in Kirsehir in central Turkey and accepted people into the profession. The symbolic entrance ceremony involved girding the candidate, thereby approving his qualification to be a member of the profession. Later, the head of the tanners in Kirsehir became the head of all the professions with the support of the Sultan, who benefited from the contributions of *Ahi* organizations during both war and peace. During war time some *Ahi* organizations produced manpower for the army and made guns. During peace time, *Ahi* organizations contributed to the material and social betterment of society.

---

[21] For more information, see: www.tr.wikipedia.org/vakiflargenel mudurlugu (11.05.2008),

http://www.vakifbank.com.tr/vakifbank-tarihcesi.aspx or http://www.diyanet-sen.org.tr/article.php?article_id=8. (accessed 11.05.2008).

[22] Cahen C. "Futuwwa." *Encyclopedia of Islam (EI-2)*.

Although *Ahis* never had independent political power, they played roles which the state would normally undertake, such as defending the cities and towns against Mongol invasion. In some instances, they played an intermediary role between the state and the masses.[23] These organizations were, in a sense, the equivalent of modern trade associations with a moral and spiritual dimension. They did not consider themselves to be only producers or artisans but also leaders responsible for the wellbeing of the community, both materially and socially. The members of these organizations were expected to display the following qualities: loyalty, trustworthiness, generosity, justice, modesty, helpfulness to their fellow professionals and willingness to forgive.

Bereket

Another important concept that is part of Turkish–Islamic philanthropy is the concept of *bereket.* The word means "beneficial force, of divine origin, which causes superabundance in the physical sphere and prosperity and happiness in the psychic order."[24] The word "*bereket*" has become an integral part of Turkish culture and is used in everyday Turkish. Indeed, the majority of Turks believe that when something is done with the intent of pleasing God and without expectation of worldly reward, it will create abundance. For example, if an individual gives a portion of his or her money to the poor or needy, he/she expects that the rest of that money will become abundant (i.e., more than enough to meet the individual's needs). This idea of abundance resulting from generosity is applied not only to money, but also to time, life and other tangible objects, such as crops, food and so on. It is believed that if an individual commits a portion of his time to a good deed, he will be more efficient and productive in using the remainder of his time.

This concept of *bereket* has its root in the Qur'an, which says:

> Those men and women who give alms (by spending out of their wealth in both the prescribed and supererogatory duties of almsgiving) and lend to God a goodly loan (by spending either in His cause or for the needy), it will be increased manifold to their credit, and they will have an honorable, generous reward in addition (57:18)[25]

Bereket is a word used commonly in everyday Turkish life, whether or not the speaker holds a particularly religious worldview. For example, after completing a business transaction, store owners or salesmen say, "May Allah make it abundant" ("*Allah bereket versin*"), while putting the money in their pockets or into the cash

---

[23] Ergun (1922).

[24] Collin (1960).

[25] See also: Quran 64:18 which says "If ye loan to Allah, a beautiful loan, He will double it to your (credit), and He will grant you Forgiveness: for Allah is most Ready to appreciate (service), Most Forbearing."

register. In more rural areas, when a person visits a neighbor in the process of harvesting, he or she says, "Let it be abundant!" ("*Bereketli olsun*").[26]

In addition, the Prophet Abraham is considered to be an important model of generosity and hospitality. Folk legend has it that he had a house with four gates. All of the gates were kept open; and people would come from every direction to partake of his table. He always had guests and his table was always full. Turks believe, accordingly, that guests bring abundance and blessings to the host. Numerous linguistic expressions indicate this belief. For example, after dining in someone else's home, Turks say, "Let this table be like the table of Abraham!", meaning let it be rewarded with wealth and blessings. As one travels through Turkey's cities and towns, one also sees many restaurants called "Abraham's Table" ("*Halil İbrahim Sofrası*").

Komsuluk (Neighborliness)

Generosity and good relations with neighbors are also of utmost importance in Turkish–Islamic culture. Many Turks are aware that the Prophet Muhammad emphasized the importance of having good relations with neighbors and can cite prophetic traditions such as: "The Prophet said, "Gabriel continued to recommend that I treat my neighbors kindly and politely so often that I thought he would order me to make them my heirs"[27] and

> Allah's Apostle said, 'Anybody who believes in Allah and the Last Day should not harm his neighbor, and anybody who believes in Allah and the Last Day should entertain his guest generously and anybody who believes in Allah and the Last Day should talk what is good or keep quiet (i.e., abstain from all kinds of evil and dirty talk).[28]

Muslim scholars unanimously agree that non-Muslim neighbors have the same rights as Muslim neighbors since no prophetic traditions specifically mention Muslim neighbors, and some traditions relate incidents of the Prophet Muhammad's or his family members' generosity toward Jewish neighbors.[29]

In the modern Turkish language, various proverbs indicate the high value of good neighbors. These include: "Don't buy a house, acquire a neighbor!" ("*Ev alma, komşu al!*") and "A neighbor might need even the ash of his neighbor" ("*Komşu komşunun külüne muhtaçtı.*"). Accordingly, most Turks make an effort to

[26] Other phrases in the Turkish language describe how abundance or blessings have been cut off ("*Bet bereket kesildi.*") or have ended ("*Bereket kalktı.*") due to a person's lack of generosity). The variety of common phrases using the word "*bereket*" indicate that this concept has become an integral part of Turkish culture.

[27] Al-Bukhârî, Adab, 28. *Riyâd-us-Sâliheen* (1991).

[28] Sahih Bukhari, Volume 8, Book 73, No. 47.

[29] Diyanet İslam Ansiklopedisi, "Komşu," p. 157.

keep good relations with their neighbors by greeting them with a smile and engaging in short chats, by inviting them for tea or coffee, by visiting them on holidays and/ or in times of trouble, by offering them extra helpings of cookies, stuffed grape leaves or whatever has been cooked at home that day, and by keeping family noise to a minimum. Turkish housewives, in particular, tend to have closer relationships with neighboring housewives, and often share the tasks of cooking, baking and child care among themselves. They might also contribute money to a monthly "pot," given in turn to a neighbor in need, or come together on Fridays to read the Qur'an.

Karz-i-Hasen

Karz-i hasen is one last important aspect of the culture of giving in Turkey. The literal meaning of the expression is "a good loan." *Karzi-i hasen* indicates a loan which is returned without interest at the end of a period agreed on by both parties. In Turkish society, as well as other Muslim societies, giving *karzi-i hasen* to help someone meet his or her needs is considered a good deed, one rewarded by God. Various Qur'anic verses and Prophetic traditions praise interest-free lending of money to people in need. One Qur'anic verse reads: "If you lend God a goodly loan, He will increase it manifold to you and will forgive you. God is All-Responsive (to gratitude), All-Clement (forbearing before many of the faults of His servants)."[30] Accordingly, lending money for a good reason and without charging interest is regarded as having worldly benefits for the recipient and spiritual benefits for the loaner. *Karz-i hasen*, which is said to strengthen social harmony and cooperation, is still practiced by many Turks, even though Western banking is predominant in the country. For example, most Turks would prefer to pay their monthly bills or buy their cars and homes via *karzi-i hasen* from close relatives, neighbors or friends, rather than take a loan from a bank or creditor.

The Gülen Movement's Revival of Turkish–Islamic Philanthropy

As the above examples make evident, Islamic and Turkish culture have amalgamated to create a long and rich tradition of giving in Turkey. In this context it becomes easy to see that one reason for the success of the Gülen movement is its ability to gain peoples' trust by tapping into the network of philanthropic urges already present in Turkish society. For example, when Mr. Gülen outlined his vision

---

[30] Qur'an, 64:17.

of providing quality education for all Turkish youth by establishing dormitories, preparatory courses, and ultimately, high schools and universities, he called upon everyone inspired by his vision to take part in providing these opportunities for the young people in Turkey. He challenged men and women to become teachers and dedicate their lives to teaching the youth, principals to be devoted to establishing first-rate curricula and suitable environments for learning, and businessmen to expand their businesses and make them more lucrative so that they could monetarily support the activities of the movement. Furthermore, he expressed his call to action in terms of fundamental Turkish–Islamic values: hospitality, giving, charity and the obligation to help the needy in society. These ideas and the sacrifices they entailed were familiar to those who heard and heeded Gülen's call because they were embedded in the culture in which they were raised. Gülen simply provided ways in which Turks could express the generosity and giving that they were called to by the tenets of their culture and religion. In short, participants in the movement who give *sadaka* to poor students, who send their *kurban* meat to poor families in Southeast Turkey or the heart of Africa, who dedicate their careers and/or business toward good deeds (*hayır hasenat*) or who help the victims of natural disasters are motivated by the age-old traditions of charity and philanthropy in Turkish society.

The Water for the Mill: Financing
of Gülen-Inspired Service Projects

In order to build and sustain the numerous projects associated with the Gülen movement, financial resources are essential. Data presented in Chapter 4 "The Network of Local Circles" describe the mechanisms established within the local circles to generate substantial financial resources. Chapter 5 "The Turkish–Islamic Culture of Giving" presented Turkish–Islamic concepts of giving and hospitality that are deeply rooted in Turkish culture. This chapter focuses upon financial arrangements in relationship to the institutions that are associated with the Gülen movement.

In November, 2004, Mr. Gülen was asked by a reporter "where the water for this mill comes from," a Turkish expression meaning "what is the source of all the money behind the Gülen-inspired projects?" Mr. Gülen admitted that he has been asked this question many times by Turkish politicians and journalists who assume that there are self interests or hidden plans behind the movement's projects. He says that there are many people who would not give you a cup of tea without guaranteeing that they will get two cups of tea from you in return. However, Mr.Gülen contrasts these people with those who are devoted to supporting the good works inspired by his teachings. Of them, he says, "Those are our people who give and give. You could say they are addicted to giving. If you say 'not to give' to them they will be sad and unhappy." He goes on to tell the story of a retired man to whom he spoke before a fundraiser. The man could not give anything because he had very little. When Mr. Gülen was leaving the building, the man caught him on the stairs and handed him a set of keys and said, "These are the keys of my house. I don't have anything to give other than that house, please take these keys." Mr. Gülen gave back the keys and told him not to worry but to give when he had something to give. Mr. Gülen went on to praise the people of Anatolia as miraculous people who support projects that they see as worthwhile and that help to solve the problems of the world and the future of their nation. He commented that the leaders of Turkey have not been able to use this potential in their people.

Mr. Gülen himself has never had personal wealth to be able to sponsor projects. He has chosen to live an ascetic life dedicated to worship and reading. For a number of years he lived in a corner of a local mosque with barely enough space to lie

H.R. Ebaugh, *The Gülen Movement: A Sociological Analysis of a Civic Movement Rooted in Moderate Islam*, DOI 10.1007/978-1-4020-9894-9_6,
© Springer Science+Business Media B.V. 2010

down. In addition to never having any personal wealth, he prayed for his relatives to remain poor so as not to raise any suspicions of gaining from his influence.[1] He has appeared at many fund-raising dinners and visited wealthy individuals to try to convince them to support excellent and modern education. However, apart from encouraging people to donate money, Mr. Gülen has remained distanced from all financial involvements and instead has encouraged those who sponsor projects to oversee the use of their contributions. This stance has built trust and confidence in Mr. Gülen's honesty and integrity.

Gülen-Inspired Institutions

Bank Asya

Bank Asya today is the largest of the four "participation banks" in Turkey.[2] The bank opened in 1996 when 346 businessmen throughout Turkey bought shares in the bank and obtained a license from the Turkish Treasury Department to open an interest-free bank (originally called finance houses). At the time Bank Asya was one of six such banks and was known as Asya Finans. Since then one bank went into bankruptcy and two merged, leaving the current four participation banks in Turkey with Bank Asya being the largest with a 30% market share.

In what way can Bank Asya be called a Gülen-inspired bank? In the early 1990s Mr. Gülen agreed with some businessmen that opening an interest-free bank was probably a good idea. Earlier, in 1983, then President Ozal signed a decree that established special finance houses based on interest-free banking in order to serve the Muslim Turkish people who did not want to put their money into interest bearing accounts, Mr. Gülen, a friend of President Ozal, supported the decree and encouraged the original businessmen to pursue their plans to open such a bank. Some of these first businessmen were inspired by the preaching and writings of Mr. Gülen. However, this was not true of all 346 of them, some of whom were indifferent to Mr. Gülen's ideas but saw a business opportunity in the establishment of such a bank. Mr. Gülen did attend the opening ceremony of the bank and was photographed with some of the original shareholders who also attended. The media, therefore, helped create the image that this bank was associated with the Gülen movement. The more accurate representation, however, is that some of the individual shareholders were part of the movement and many were not.

---

[1] Aslandogan and Cetin (2006).

[2] For a discussion of Islamic finances, see Yousef (2004).

Some of the Gülen-inspired schools and hospitals do use Bank Asya for some of their banking needs. However, this choice is based upon competitive bidding among banks in Turkey. As the president of the bank, Mr. Unal Kabaca insisted repeatedly that the bank has to work hard to compete for all the business it has. The bank has no competitive edge with Gülen-inspired projects and has to work as hard to obtain that business as it does with other businesses in Turkey. For example, Fatih University, a Gülen-inspired institution, worked for many years with a government bank until Bank Asya won their business by developing a system of collecting tuition that appealed to the board of directors of the university. The bank issued a credit card to families of students which they can use to make monthly payments for tuition whether in grade schools, high schools or universities. This tuition credit card has been very successful and appealing to Turkish families making tuition payments. However, Bank Asya offers the same credit card service to all private schools that are interested, not only to Gülen-inspired schools. Because of its success with tuition credit cards, Bank Asya now services a number of educational institutions, including a number of local universities.

A number of the original stockholders have sold their shares in the bank so that today only 30% of shares are owned by the original group. Today the bank is public and owned by numerous individuals and companies who have bought bank shares. There is no way of knowing how many of these individuals are inspired by Mr. Gülen since the movement has no membership list and affiliation with the group is completely an individual matter. The current chairman of the board of Bank Asya is a wealthy businessman who owns several companies in the shipping industry, is a supporter of various Gülen-inspired projects and was on the board of trustees for Fatih University at one time. However, being a Gülen supporter is in no way a requirement for the position. There are no official ties between Mr. Gülen and the board of directors of the bank, the bank officers, or clients of the bank. Once every three years the general assembly of shareholders, including foreign investors, elect the president and board of directors. Most of these shareholders have never heard of Mr. Gülen or his movement. Mr. Kabaca contends that today Mr. Gülen's spirit and ideas do not have significant impact on the bank.

Mr. Kabaca described Bank Asya as an "Islamic bank" in so far as interest on one's money is not practiced at the bank; rather, the bank invests in real transactions that involve actual products rather than compounded interest on money alone. In addition, the bank does not finance gambling or alcohol. Some non-Muslim people, including Christians and Jews who are opposed to the mechanism of compounded interest for reasons other than religion, bank their money with Bank Asya, especially if their social values match those of the bank. It is also the case that the bank has performed very well, increasing its capital seven to eight times since its origins 12 years ago. In 2007, Bank Asya posted net profits of 51% and reported that funds in its profit-sharing accounts rose 47%, with current deposits of $5 billion. As a result of its financial success, the bank has attracted global investors, both individuals and companies.

During the 2002 financial crisis in Turkey, most banks would not invest in construction companies, either locally or internationally. Bank Asya saw an opportunity for growth and supported many construction companies both in the Gulf region and in Africa. This investment resulted in substantial profits for the bank and raised its visibility in the economic community worldwide. Today many shareholders are institutional, especially from the United States and Europe. Of the $5 billion in deposits, approximately $2 billion are from individuals and the remaining $3 billion from companies. Participation banks in Turkey, while having only 3.2% of the banking business in Turkey, are growing, up from 1.1% in 2001 and with a projection of 10% of the Turkish banking market in three years.

In summary, while Mr. Gülen originally supported the idea of an interest-free bank and encouraged the original businessmen to pursue their plans to open such a bank, there never were official ties between Mr. Gülen and Bank Asya. While some of the original shareholders were inspired by Mr. Gülen and his ideas, this was certainly not the case for all 346 of the original shareholders and has become less so as the bank has grown, become more competitive and successful in the marketplace and has increasingly attracted foreign investors.

Samanyolu Television Station

During the 1980s Mr. Gülen began advocating responsible media, including both newspapers and broadcasting. In 1989 he met with some twenty businessmen in Istanbul to explore the possibility of opening a television station that would be committed to balanced, objective and socially responsible reporting of news, in addition to programs that would emphasize a family orientation with no explicit sexuality or violent crime. Some member of the original group estimated that the startup cost of opening such a station would be approximately $250,000. The businessmen agreed to put up the initial capital and Samanyolu TV or STV, as viewers call it, was launched on January 13, 1993. However, the costs for opening a new station were approximately four times higher than estimated. For the first six or seven years, therefore, the station was unable to support itself with generated income and was subsidized by local businessmen who were part of the Gülen-inspired movement. However, after four to five years, the station became increasingly self supportive each year, primarily through paid advertising, and since 2004 it has required no assistance from local supporters.

Currently, the income from advertising is sufficient to cover the entire costs of operations. In fact, the station now has a profit margin that allows it to expand its programming and broadcasting venues. Its programming today includes dramas, sports, comedies, reality shows, a food preparation program, children's programming and a 24 hour news program. What differentiates Samanyolu from other Turkish television stations, according to Mr. Karakas, the Public Relations Director, is that it emphasizes a family orientation in all its programming. The station also includes programs that promote the movement's goals of intercultural and interfaith dialog.

One of its most popular programs in the recent past was "Kimse Yok Mu," or "Is anybody there?", a reality program that aired following the 2004 earthquake outside Istanbul. Relief workers who entered the devastated area rescued a little girl who was calling, "Is anybody there?" The program featured two families, one poor and one with economic resources. The wealthier family set about helping the poor family to reconstruct its life after the earthquake. As a result of the program, donations poured into the station to help the earthquake victims. As a result, the nonprofit relief organization, Kimse Yok Mu, was established to distribute the monies for the earthquake disaster and others around the country and the globe.

Samanyolu T.V.'s cooking show, *Yesil Elma* or the Green Apple, ranks #1 among such programs in Turkey and *Tek Turkiye*, a series show, became the top most frequently viewed show in the country in 2008. Beginning in 1998, AGB, a central company that ranks stations on the basis of 2,500 different measurements, began recommending Samanyolu TV to advertisers. The fact that the station broadcasts in many different languages and airs in many different regions of the world by means of satellite is appealing to many international businesses and has resulted in robust advertising for the television station, resulting in Samanyolu becoming a profitable business. Today Samanyolu T.V. has a yearly budget of about $36 million or $3 million per month.

Zaman Newspaper

In the mid 1980s, Mr. Gülen and some of those around him who supported his ideology thought that it was a good idea to have a newspaper that would be inclusive in terms of reporting various ideological perspectives and opinions, would report the most current news in an objective fashion, would emphasize dialog and tolerance rather than hatred among groups and that would deemphasize alcohol and nudity in its advertising. In 1986 a group of Turkish businessmen who were inspired by Mr. Gülen and who thought that a newspaper with such goals was a good business venture bought shares in the paper and thus *Zaman* was launched.

It was businessmen interested in the media who owned and controlled the paper from its inception. Even though some of the original shareholders were influenced and inspired by Mr. Gülen, he himself had no financial nor administrative involvement in the paper. He never served on its board or in its corporate structure even though he writes a column in *Zaman* every Friday.

The Editor-in-Chief of *Zaman*, Mr. Ehrem Dumanli, expressed the goal of *Zaman* as follows: "We are trying to produce a paper at world standards. This is our standard; not to have it produce a propagandist piece of paper to attract some new members to the community. We want to have a paper that can compete with other papers so we like for *Zaman* to be read as the best paper so we encourage our staff to bring us the best news." Today, 22 years after its beginnings, *Zaman* has the largest circulation of any newspaper in Turkey with an average of 760,000 daily paid subscriptions and a total readership estimated at two and a half million people per day (this includes those who share subscriptions and who buy the paper from newsstands).

In addition to *Zaman*, the Turkish version of the newspaper, and *Zaman Today*, the English version, there is a larger Media Group of which the papers are one part. In addition, the Media Group includes a weekly magazine and a news agency. In 2007 the income for the Media Group was approximately $250 million, with over half of that coming from subscriptions. However, for the newspapers, over 50% of income comes from advertising and less from subscriptions. Advertizing comes mostly from mainstream businesses that want to reach a broad audience and are not associated with the Gülen movement in any way. As Mr. Dumanli explained, "These businesses just want good business and see our paper as a way of reaching their desired market."

Today *Zaman* is not only self supportive but is a profitable business venture for its shareholders. Currently, the largest shareholder in *Zaman* is a wealthy textile manufacturer in Turkey. Mr. Dumanli was unsure how many of the current board of directors are affiliated with the Gülen movement. He said that the board is chosen from leaders in the media and business community of Turkey with no stipulation of ties to the movement.

When asked how the current paper reflects the ideas of Mr. Gülen, Mr. Dumanli said that without Mr. Gülen's influence in terms of shared ideas, "we would not be able to produce the paper because we have Gülen's idea of dialog across cultures and religions so that the paper reflects a variety of opinions which is hard to see in other papers. Most are ideological. We try to reflect different opinions, especially in the columnists. Opinion pages are open to anyone and do not include hatred of anyone." He continued to say that columnists come from both the right and the left and that views on issues come from all sides of the spectrum. Free expression of opinion, regardless of religion or ethnic group, is carefully guarded in the policies of the paper. In Mr. Dumanli's opinion, these policies defending freedom of speech is what makes *Zaman* successful. While there are no "Gülen classes" or formalized mechanisms for socializing *Zaman* staff to the ideas of Mr. Gülen, there is a general atmosphere that incorporates Gülen's basic principles of dialog, tolerance, freedom of expression, commitment to democracy and inclusiveness.

Financial transparency is one of the requisites of *Zaman*'s staying in business. Every year the government investigates the finances of every newspaper and if there are any infringements in regard to financial operations or transparency, the paper can be shut down or fined. In its 22 year history, *Zaman* has had no infringements despite the rigorous review by financial auditors.

In summary, *Zaman* is a Gülen-inspired newspaper in so far as some of the original shareholders were inspired by Mr. Gülen's ideas and the fact that he encouraged its instigation. In addition, the paper is committed to Gülen notions of dialog, the representation of various opinions and hatred of no one. Also, advertising is limited to ads that do not promote nudity, alcohol or crime related activities. However, there is no financial link between the paper and the Gülen movement. It is a profit making business venture for its shareholders.

The Journalists and Writers Foundation

During a visit to Istanbul in 1994, Mr. Gülen met with a group of writers and journalists and said that they had an important educational role to play in shaping ideas of the public, especially in regard to dialog between cultures, ethnicities and religions. His remarks came a decade or so after strong polarization among intellectuals in Turkey, resulting in some actual instances of armed conflict. The increasing polarization among communists, nationalists and radical religious groups in Turkey and the brutal war in Bosnia–Herzegovina were the backdrop for Mr. Gülen's insistence that dialog among cultures, civilizations and religions was more needed than ever in Turkey and in the world. Mr. Gülen encouraged the group to bring people with different ideologies to the same table for dialog and encouraged them to create a foundation that would be devoted to this purpose.

In June1994, a core group of writers and journalists who had met with Mr. Gülen and were inspired by his vision of a dialog foundation initiated the Journalists and Writers Foundation with headquarters in Istanbul. Mr. Gülen agreed to serve as honorary president of the foundation, a role he performed for the first 10 years or so of the foundation. At the core of the Foundation are the Abant Platform Meetings, a venue for debate that highlights different perspectives on the solutions to common challenges and also the fundamental human values that participants share. For example, these meetings have brought together Turks of diverse intellectual and religious backgrounds, including Muslims, secularists, traditionalists, modernists, atheists, Christians, leftists and conservatives, to discuss and debate common positions on key contemporary issues. The Abant platform statements that result from these meetings outline points of common agreement.

The major funding for the foundation comes from their publishing unit, books that cater primarily to intellectuals. While many publishers report sales of 2,000 or so copies of a book, the Foundation has sold over 50,000 copies of some books, especially those written by Mr. Gülen. From their publications, the Foundation makes between \$300,000–500,000 per year. The sale of musical CDs has also garnered some revenue, albeit minimal in most years. When organizing a specific event such as an Abant Platform Meeting or conference on a specific topic, the Foundation approaches local businessmen for support. On three occasions, the Foundation did receive government grants to cover the costs of bringing scholars from other countries, totaling less than \$50,000. In addition, the Foundation has initiated some innovative projects as a way to generate money. The latest was the production of a CD by a famous singer who agreed to donate proceeds for tutoring centers in poor areas within Turkey and the world. In addition, the Foundation was able to get ten well known singers in Turkey, none of them deeply involved in the movement, to donate their renditions of songs for a CD which has already sold 200,000 in a short time period. The proceeds of these efforts help support the work of the Foundation.

Another fund raising project involved the Foundation's sponsoring of a soccer match between Turkish national athletes and other world famous athletes.

The money raised by the event was used to set up schools in Bosnia for Serb and Bosnian students. The usual Serb/Bosnian conflict stopped at the school doors due to the fact that children from both ethnic groups attended the school with the goal of getting a good education.

Because of its status as a legal foundation, the Journalists and Writers Foundation is eligible for property tax advantages on property that it owns for business use. However, the group currently rents space and can therefore not take advantage of this tax cut. In many years the Foundation ends the year in debt. However, due to Mr. Gülen's latest book that it published and which has been very successful in terms of sales, the Foundation plans to buy property soon to house their offices.

Fatih University

Fatih University opened in 1994, one year after Congress approved the request for a private university to be built on the outskirts of Istanbul. In Turkey only charitable foundations can establish private universities, not individuals or businesses for the purpose of profit. The "founding foundation" that initially financed Fatih was located in Ankara and consisted of supporters who were associated with the Gülen movement. The finances came from Gülen supporters in two cities: Ankara businessmen who pledged money to build and support the university and also Istanbul businessmen. One wealthy businessman from Istanbul donated the scenic property on which the university is located, appraised at the time at approximately $5 million. Today the property is worth about $100 million. Once the land was donated, other businessmen contributed to constructing the buildings and the initial opening of the university.

Currently, tuition fees are sufficient to run the university in terms of operating costs, including maintenance of buildings, faculty salaries, etc. However, Turkish law says that buildings cannot be constructed with tuition money but that foundations must raise the money for such expenditures. Each of the university buildings and labs, therefore, was built by donations collected by the foundation. Several years ago the foundation built a lab that cost about $7 million; in 2007 the university finished its preparatory course building that cost about $4 million. In 2008 the university needs $15 million to build labs but the foundation says it cannot raise that much money in one year so it will give half this year and half next year.

Many people, mostly Gülen supporters, make contributions to the foundation. There are a small number of very wealthy individuals who make large contributions and the university often names a building or lab in honor of such donors. However, the foundation and the university are extremely careful in terms of accepting donations, with the intention of not accepting money from radical political groups. Recently the University was in urgent need of several new science buildings and had the opportunity to apply for a development grant from an Islamic bank that offers interest-free monies to universities in Muslim countries in order to promote education. The bank is located in Saudi Arabia and the money is obtained through the Turkish government. University officials took the proposal to Mr. Gülen and he strongly urged them not to pursue the loan. As he said, given the fact that the bank is located in Saudi Arabia, people will accuse the movement of accepting Saudi money, something that he is insistent is not a good idea. He counseled the officials to just wait, be patient, and get the money from the Gülen community in Turkey.

According to the law of higher education in Turkey, if a university meets certain criteria, the government gives it 15% of its budget every year. This is allocated to each and every qualifying university in Turkey. In 2006 and 2007, Fatih qualified and received its portion; in 2008 it failed on one criterion and was denied the assistance.

The relationship between the foundation and the university is strictly monetary. In fact, university officials do not know who serves on the foundation board. The Vice-Rector whom I interviewed told a story to demonstrate this fact. Recently he was at a meeting in Istanbul and mentioned that the university needed more land for expansion. A gentleman in the group whom he did not know remarked, "You mean that land I gave you originally is not enough?" It was just accidentally that he met the original donor. Likewise, university administrators are not aware of who serves on the foundation board or who contributes to the foundation. Monies are given to the foundation which supports the university among many other projects. When people give to the foundation, routinely they are uncertain which of the projects will be funded with their donations.

The foundation has no control over the university other than providing funds for specific projects when asked by the university administration. No one from the foundation routinely sits on the board of trustees of the university or has input into the academic affairs of the university. This is also true for most individual donors who give to the university. For example, the owner of a major jewelry company donated money for a building on campus, came for the opening of the building and was never seen again by administrators at Fatih.

When asked what percentage of Fatih's students are participants in the Gülen movement, Dr. Acikgenc, the Vice-Rector of the university, estimated that perhaps 50% are sympathizers, meaning that they are involved at different levels in the movement. Fatih University is well known as Gülen-related so the choice to attend Fatih usually indicates at least that the student is not hostile to the Gülen movement. There is no religious studies department at the university, no courses on Mr. Gülen or his ideas, no pictures or statues of him, or any organized circles or discussions that focus on his teachings. Any local circles of students that meet to discuss Mr. Gülen's works are totally informal and voluntary. There is a preference to hire administrators who are inspired by Mr. Gülen so that they can maintain the mission of the university in the spirit of Mr. Gülen. Among faculty, however, less than 50% are from the movement. Fatih tries to hire faculty who share the values espoused by Mr. Gülen of inclusiveness, dialog, respect for education and science, and preparing students in a humanistic fashion to respect each other and to be good citizens who are respectful of their country.

At Fatih University the Turkish law of no alcohol on campus is strictly enforced which is not the case on many campuses. For that reason, many Turkish families favor sending their daughters to Fatih. The expectation is that girls are safe here and under stricter supervision than in many other Turkish universities. As a result, Fatih has more women students in attendance than in many other universities.

Gülen-Inspired Hospitals

There are six Gülen-inspired hospitals in Turkey. We visited two of them, Sema Hospital in Istanbul and Bahar Hospital in Bursa. Sema Hospital was initially financed by five businessmen from the Gülen community who wanted to initiate a project in the health care sector. They discussed with Mr. Gülen the idea of taking the highly successful educational model for Gülen-inspired schools and applying it to opening a private hospital. Mr. Gülen supported the idea and encouraged them to proceed with their plans. The original five businessmen provided the initial funding for Sema Hospital from personal funds and money that they were able to borrow because of their financial leverage with banks in Istanbul. The original five businessmen are still on the board of trustees of the hospital and remain closely involved in its operations.

Even though Turkey has universal health care, it does not cover all expenses incurred in private hospitals. For some medical conditions, such as heart problems, intensive care and eye treatment, the hospital does not charge beyond the amount provided by universal health care. For other out-of-pocket charges, some people are able to pay privately and others cannot. For the latter patients, often their medical bills are taken care of by Gülen sponsors. Sometimes a sponsor will accompany a patient and ask that charges above and beyond insurance be sent to him or her for payment. In other instances, sponsors send money anonymously to help needy patients and hospital personnel do not know who they are. In still other cases, patients come to the hospital needing care but admit up front that they are not able to pay beyond their government health care plan. In those instances, hospital personnel will try to find a sponsor who is willing to assist that particular patient. Kristin, the Public Health Administrator of the hospital, a Harvard graduate, commented,

> "We have an amazing network of people who sponsor patients who come to us for care. They sponsor our patients. The system is very informal but it works. The Gülen Movement is very effective in being aware we are a new hospital and we need to get our feet on the ground. The sponsors do not want us to have to delay our achievements so they are very generous in their support."

In the strategic plan of Sema Hospital, there are no financial goals. Rather, the emphasis is on employee and patient satisfaction. Because it is private, Sema Hospital is a for-profit hospital; however, profits do not go to the original businessmen to enhance their financial portfolios. Rather, profit goes into improving and expanding the hospital, providing more care for the poor or helping other hospitals to get started and succeed. Several times in the course of the interview with Kristen and a group of doctors, the comment was made that if Sema Hospital can develop a model that works, other hospitals will be built by Gülen supporters and thus many more needy people will be served in an atmosphere of humane and caring treatment.

Sema Hospital differs from other hospitals, both public and private, in three basic ways: (1) the way doctors and staff are hired and paid; (2) its pricing strategy; and (3) the way patients are treated. In many public hospitals, doctors are civil servants and are very busy. As one doctor commented, "Often in public hospitals, doctors treat patients as a nuisance." The doctor continued, "There is something different in this hospital. People work not for the money but for the patients." The hiring process at Sema Hospital is rigid. While credentials and experience are important for both medical and non-medical staff, recruiters and hiring personnel also look "more at what people are made of than what they have done. A nurse who enjoys helping people may be more beneficial to patients than a highly trained nurse who does not like people." One of the doctors commented that many of the 80 physicians at Sema belong to local Gülen circles before they are hired and others may not be involved in the movement but want to work in a place that is humanizing and based on the Gülen school model. Frequently, the doctors take a pay cut to work at Sema Hospital but their desire to be part of a staff that prioritizes patient care in a supportive atmosphere outweighs financial concerns. Likewise, other medical and non-medical staff, as well, know that Sema is a Gülen-inspired hospital and would not opt to work there if he or she was not compatible with the culture and atmosphere of the hospital.

Of the 20,000 physicians employed in Istanbul, about 2,000 are connected with the Gülen movement and are part of local circles of physicians. At their own expense, in April, 2008, 60 doctors connected to the Gülen Movement, went to Southeast Turkey to see patients at no cost for three days. About 130 of these patients, most of them with cardiac problems, were transported back to Sema Hospital and treated free of charge. In addition, the circles of doctors committed to the Gülen movement all give money to the movement, as do many of the employees at the hospital. In fact, the employees at Sema support a Gülen-inspired school in Albania.

Sema Hospital also cares for teachers in all the Gülen-inspired schools anywhere in the world at the same billing scale as hospital employees which is 80% reduction of usual fees. In addition to assisting these teachers who often work for minimal wages and cannot afford additional health care insurance, as Kristin mentioned, "We want to honor them for the work they are doing." For example, the day before our interview a teacher from a Gülen-inspired school in Nigeria came for treatment for multiple diseases. In gratitude for the care that Sema Hospital was offering this patient, the minister from Nigeria promised land for a Gülen-inspired hospital in Nigeria. One of the doctors we interviewed said that some doctors among the group of physicians who visited southeast Turkey to provide medical care were planning to also visit Africa to determine if it would be feasible to open hospitals there based on the model of Gülen schools that was now successfully being used at Sema Hospital. In fact, he said that an ideal scenario would be to train doctors and nurses in the Gülen educational system and then hire them in Gülen-related hospitals so that the spirit and goals inspired by Mr. Gülen would permeate these various institutions.

In terms of how patients experience the unique atmosphere in Sema Hospital, Kristen gave the example of a blue-collar worker who said after heart surgery: "I learned here I am human. I didn't understand my value as a human being until I came here." She said the hospital has many such testimonies of how patient care is different than in many other hospitals. Some patients from within Turkey and from other countries come to Sema precisely because they know it is a Gülen-inspired hospital. Others come because they have heard that the hospital provides top notch care in an atmosphere that respects the patient as a human being.

Bahar Hospital, Bursa

Bahar Hospital started as a medical center in 1998 when a group of businessmen hired 4–5 doctors to run a small medical clinic. In addition to the businessmen, there was grassroots support from many Gülen movement participants in Bursa who were inspired to have a medical center. The first ambulance was purchased with money from some jewelry donated by women supporters. In 2004 the first floor of the building was opened as a hospital. On the top floor of the eight floor building was a Gülen school which subsequently moved out so that the hospital could expand. Today the hospital spans all eight floors with 80 patient beds. There are currently 53 physicians and 400 total personnel in the hospital.

Throughout the units of the hospital is state-of-the-art medical equipment, including a highly rated cardio-vascular unit in which over 700 cardiac surgeries have been performed. Of the eight private hospitals in the city, Bahar Hospital is the third largest, performing about 1,000 surgeries every month with an annual budget of approximately $40 million and a profit rate of 10–15%.

The motto of Bahar Hospital is: "Trust in medicine." Often in Turkey patients suspect that the doctors prescribe procedures and medicines for profit motives rather than the best interest of the patient. A major feature of Bahar Hospital is to give trust to their patients. For example, recently a patient went to see an eye doctor in Istanbul for an opinion on an eye condition and was suspicious of the diagnosis so came to Bahar on the advice of a friend who said that at Bahar she could trust the doctors.

Bahar insists that its staff treat patients like family members and make them feel "at home" in the hospital atmosphere. Staff, including doctors, are hired on the basis of both professional competency and attitudes toward patient care. About 40% of the general personnel are Gülen movement participants; the other 60% are not part of the movement but share the value of putting the health care of the patient foremost.

The hospital has a capacity for patients who cannot pay. Twice in recent months doctors from the hospital went to southeast Turkey and found patients who needed surgery and brought them to Bahar for treatment. These patients were not charged for services. Under the leadership of the hospital there is an association that attracts doctors who want to do good works, similar to Doctors Across Borders.

Most of these doctors are part of the Gülen movement. The association sent 35 doctors from Bursa to one city in southeast Turkey and 40 to another city.

The pay scale of the doctors is in line with the median salaries of physicians in the private sector. The hospital insists that doctors be paid adequately so that they do not have to be concerned with their salaries and can focus on good patient care. In addition, many of the doctors in the hospital belong to local circles of physicians and through these circles pledge financial support for various projects, including health care projects but also schools and student scholarships. For example, one doctor we interviewed makes approximately $120,000 per year, has three children and personally pledges 30% of his annual income to Gülen-inspired projects, a sum that totals a contribution of about $40,000 per year. He says that he has known doctors who pledge 50% of their annual salaries to these projects. He estimated that donations from doctors in Bursa support about 600 scholarships a year, each worth $1,500 for a total donation of $900,000 per year. In addition, he said that the doctors also support specific school buildings and other projects as they arise.

When asked why he makes such a contribution, he remarked,

> "I see this as being thankful to God. This mentality began in me when I was staying in the homes where students were staying. I had gratitude. I also saw businessmen giving big amounts and I wanted to give in these amounts when I had a chance. So I believe it is pleasing to God and He rewards those who act according to His wish."

In medical school, this doctor stayed in student dormitories and homes and he noticed that the amount of money he paid was not sufficient to run the home. He saw families inviting the students for dinner and he wondered where the money was coming from for such activities. Then he saw businessmen supporting these homes, dinners and other projects and thought that someday he wanted to be on the giving side.

Educational Institutions: Dormitories and College Preparatory Courses

At the heart of Mr. Gülen's teachings is his emphasis on the need for quality education for all Turkish youth. He sees education as the primary solution to the three problems that plague developing countries, namely, ignorance, poverty and internal schism.[3] He goes on to argue that knowledge, work-capital and unification can struggle against these. He saw ignorance as the most serious of these problems and education as the most important need in Turkish society. He argued that every problem in human life ultimately depends on human beings themselves and therefore education is the most effective vehicle regardless of whether a society has a paralyzed social and political system or one operating with clockwise precision. Mr. Gülen encouraged people to serve their country and humanity in general through promoting and supporting education.

---

[3] Unal and Williams (2003).

Along with constantly promoting education in his sermons, Mr. Gülen encouraged businessmen, powerful industrialists along with small businessmen, to financially support quality education. He realized that preparing excellent teachers was a first critical step toward superior education in the schools but that such a goal required time to achieve. Therefore, as a first step, he encouraged business owners and entrepreneurs to support dormitories where students could stay and study together under the tutelage of dedicated teachers. This arrangement was especially critical for rural youth who applied to high schools and universities in the larger cities but could not afford room and board in addition to tuition and books. In addition to providing living arrangements, these dormitories provided tutors to assist the youth staying there with their academic courses.

Mr. Gülen himself, during the 1970s, tutored youth in some of these dormitories as well as in his own apartment. Mr. Yavuz, a man in Bursa now in his seventies, recalls renting an apartment with his brother and subleasing the top floor to Mr. Gülen who constantly invited students to his apartment in order to tutor them. He also encouraged other students to tutor those who were not performing well in their classes.

Forty years later, in April 2008 when I was conducting research in Turkey, Gülen-inspired dormitories continue to proliferate throughout the country with numerous of them in each city. These dormitories are sponsored by local businessmen, professionals and workers associated with the movement. While minimal fees are charged for residents, many students cannot afford the fees and require subsidies. Few of the dormitories are totally independent financially and most depend on support from local sponsors. As evident in Chapter 4, "The Network of Local Circles", many local circles sponsor students in Gülen-related dormitories and many participants in the local circles in which I interviewed first encountered the Gülen movement in a dormitory in which they lived during high school or, more frequently, while attending university or medical school.

In addition to promoting the establishment of dormitories, a second project encouraged by Mr. Gülen was setting up college-preparatory courses to prepare high schools students for the exam that is mandatory for all students who wish to attend university. For the approximately two million high school seniors who take the exam each year, about 25% who do not take a preparatory course pass the exam. That number increases to about 50% for those who enroll in state supported courses or those privately provided. Currently, Prep courses, as they are called, supported and staffed by educators who share Gülen's educational philosophy exist in almost every city throughout Turkey. Students who attend these prep courses, on average, enhance their scores such that 75–80% pass the exam. One reason for the success of these courses is the quality and commitment of teachers who staff the courses, many of them part of the Gülen movement and motivated by reasons beyond simply financial compensation.

While the Gülen-inspired prep courses are now owned and administered as a business enterprise which charges fees, there are students who want to attend these classes but cannot afford the tuition. All of the local circles we visited provide scholarships for needy students to attend the prep courses. Such support provides opportunity for students who otherwise might not be able to obtain quality preparation for the exam. Many participants in local circles also first experienced the Gülen movement while attending a prep course. Both dormitories and prep courses, therefore, both provide educational opportunities for Turkish youth and serve, perhaps not intentionally, as a recruiting mechanism for movement participation.

Educational Institutions: Gülen-Inspired Schools

The centerpiece of the Gülen movement are the Gülen-inspired schools (estimated to be over 1,000) that exist throughout Turkey and in approximately 100 countries throughout the world, located on 5 continents. It is in these schools that Mr. Gülen's philosophy of education is most clearly expressed and where results of his educational ideas are most evident. The goal of the schools is the creation of scientifically competitive generations who will also be faithful believers and loyal citizens. Their aim is to overcome the presumed conflict between the Muslim faith, Turkish–Islamic ways of life and Western science.[4]

The schools are usually referred to as "Gülen schools," even though they are not owned by Fethullah Gülen but by private companies and institutions established by businessmen who are inspired by Mr. Gülen and share his ideas. Gülen, himself, has very little, if any, contact with the schools and is not even aware of their exact number or their names.[5] His own early example as an educator, as well as his ideas about education, global community and human progress have inspired a generation of people to build schools all over Turkey, Central Asia, Europe, Africa and elsewhere, built on the ideals of Fethullah Gülen. It is in this way that the schools are known as Gülen schools.

Like all the other Gülen-inspired institutions (e.g. the media organizations, hospitals, dormitories, prep courses), there is no central organization or formal structure that administers and oversees the schools. Rather, each school is begun by a group of businessmen and other participants in the Gülen movement who see the need for such a school in a local area and initiate the fundraising and plans to make it happen. In numerous interviews, I heard repeatedly that within Turkey there is no government support for the building, renovation or maintenance of the schools. Rather, financial support comes initially from local sponsors until the time when tuition and fees from students can make the schools self supportive.

The Gülen schools are fee-paying private schools with rigorous academic standards for admittance. It this way they are elite schools in which students tend to score high in academic achievement such as entrance into university and success in national and international scholastic competitions. The schools follow the curriculum of the host country with a majority of subjects taught in English along with some Turkish.

---

[4] Turam (2004).

[5] Carroll (2007).

Along with their fee paying structure, however, parents who pay tuition and business owners supporting the schools offer educational opportunities to some students who come from economically disadvantaged backgrounds. Approximately 20–40% of the student body in each school receives need-based scholarships. Parents, therefore, understand that the tuition they pay for their own children helps some financially needy students as well. Some parents and business sponsors also establish additional scholarships for needy students.

In Turkey the state curriculum is a totally secular one with only one hour a week of religious education required of all schools. The Gülen schools follow this model and in the one hour of required instruction in religion, they not only focus on Islam but familiarize students with other religions as well.

What differentiates the Gülen schools from other private and state schools are several factors. First, they emphasize ethical and moral values. Islam for Mr. Gülen is essentially about ethical values and the Gülen schools see themselves as faithful to Islam because they provide guidance and moral example to the students.[6] Secondly, the teachers in the schools are specially selected and trained in the notion of *temsil* or representation. Rather than preaching Islam in the schools, the teachers are role models for the students in their good deeds and moral conduct. Moreover, the commitment of the teachers to the educational and moral development of the students extends beyond the normal school day. It is not unusual for teachers to stay for many hours after the school day is over to tutor and work with students. They also work closely with the families of students, often visiting them in their homes to discuss a student's progress or problems that have arisen.

The teachers are carefully selected and are usually recruited within *cemaat* circles. Frequently, the teachers have been educated in Gülen schools and many of them have stayed in student residences or houses of light. In addition to being competent in his or her particular subject, therefore, teachers are familiar with and committed to the ideals of the Gülen movement.

Mr. Gülen continuously encouraged college students to choose education as their profession and promoted a career in education as superior to one in medicine, engineering or law, despite the prospects of a wealthier future in careers outside of education.[7] He taught that serving young people through education is a duty for every responsible human being and fulfills the purpose of man's creation. With such motivation, Mr. Gülen raised the status of teacher from a relatively low-paid, unappreciated profession to one "recognized as the key builders of the country's future."[8] As a result of the value he placed on teachers, many young people major in education and Gülen followers, in general, respect those who opt to devote their careers to education. It is the cadre of dedicated teachers that is the major hallmark of the Gülen schools and the major factor that explains their success. The fact that

---

[6] Solberg (2005).

[7] Aslandogan and Cetin (2006).

[8] Ibid.

teachers are willing to sacrifice other potentially more lucrative professions to go into education also motivates local businessmen and entrepreneurs to do their part by financially supporting the schools.

In most instances, local businessmen donate money to build a school. In addition, often in-kind donations are provided, especially on the part of supporters in the construction and furniture businesses. For example, the first Gülen school in Bursa was a high school built in the early 1980s. The group of businessmen there whom I interviewed indicated that they saw the great need for a school since government schools were inadequate. However, it was very difficult for the first 20 of them who got together to build and support the school since most of them were getting their own businesses off the ground. However, one of them pledged to buy the iron needed in the building and another provided the cement. They then sought out their friends in other industries to provide whatever materials they could to the school construction project. In this way, they built the school for one third or one half of what it would have otherwise cost. The school in which we gathered with the businessmen in Bursa, they estimated, was worth about $14 million. For this school, they successfully solicited cash donations. The men were currently involved in building a new school on the outskirts of Bursa. One of them had donated the land for the school; another was financing one of the three buildings involved and another businessmen who was not present was also paying for the construction of a second building.

When the first dormitories, prep courses and Gülen schools were established, nongovernmental foundations were established in order to raise and distribute funds to the various Gülen-inspired projects. Usually, donors were not aware of the precise projects or specific students funded by their contributions. The money was given to the foundation and then distributed to projects as needed. However, within the past decade the mechanism of setting up foundations has been abandoned in favor of setting up businesses to administer the fundraising operations that support various of the Gülen projects. The reason underlying the shift from foundation to business model relates to the fact that foundations are more strictly regulated than businesses and the fact that past military coups in Turkey resulted in new governmental agencies disbanding foundations and usurping financial resources. During unstable political eras, businesses are safer from being taken over than foundations. Even though these businesses, unlike foundations, are excluded from any tax breaks from the government, business leaders in the movement are convinced that the safety factor outweighs the tax breaks. As businesses, the companies can also make profits but these profits are routinely used to support more schools. In fact, the companies that run the Gülen schools are so successful financially that for-profit companies not associated with the movement have used the model to begin private schools. However, these schools never became as successful because the Gülen schools rely on their dedicated educators, not their tuition, for their success.

Occasionally, a wealthy businessman, like one I interviewed in Kayseri, donates enough money to build a dorm or a school single-handedly. However, few people are able to do that and the majority of projects are built by a collaborative effort on the part of many followers making contributions.

The Bursa businessmen estimated that in Bursa now there are about 1,000 people who attend local circle meetings and are constantly involved in local projects, with another 1,000 who help with specific projects. For the first group, those centrally involved with the movement, the average yearly contribution to projects is between 15% and 20%. For those who have been with the movement for a long time, the pattern is to allocate one-third of yearly income for one's business, one-third for family needs and one-third for Gülen-inspired projects. Given the fact that currently there are many wealthy business owners in Bursa who are movement participants, this amount is significant. For example, one of the businessmen in the focus group was owner and CEO of a major fabric manufacturing company and another owns a global construction company.

Estimates on the number of Gülen schools in Turkey and elsewhere vary greatly. Baskan estimates that there are 2,000 schools in 52 countries in 5 continents.[9] Balci contends that the movement has 29 schools in Kazakhstan, 12 schools in Azerbaijan, 13 in Turkmenistan and 12 schools in Kyrgyzstan. The only Turkish Central Asian country which has been hostile to the movement's schools is Uzbekistan.[10] There are schools in every Muslim country except Iran, Saudi Arabia and Libya. Six schools in Afghanistan were closed by the Taliban but are now reopened. The four schools in northern Iraq have mostly Kurd and local Muslim students.

It is impossible to give exact figures regarding the number of Gülen schools both in Turkey and now around the world for several reasons. First, there exists no centralized agency or organizational structure that controls the schools. Each of them is locally owned, financed and operated. Even within Turkey, much less globally, there is no controlling or even coordinating agency that keeps track of the schools. Secondly, it is difficult to define a Gülen school since there are numerous ways in which these schools are structured and how they relate to school systems in their locales.

In some countries outside Turkey, Gülen schools receive some government support, especially initially, in terms of land and buildings donated by the local government as a way to encourage the establishment of such a school in the country. Often, however, as a number of businessmen commented, the buildings consist of dilapidated structures that require substantial renovation. In Azerbaijan, for example, the government gave a building to use for a school. However, it needed $500,000 worth of renovations to update it which Turkish people provided. After 3 years of operation, the school was self supporting. When the first schools were opened in the Turkish countries of the former Soviet Union, Mr. Gülen asked Mr. Ozal, the president of Turkey at the time, to write letters to the governments in these countries requesting permission to open schools there. Mr. Ozal complied with the request, thus offering support for the expansion of the schools outside Turkey.

---

[9] Baskan (2004).
[10] Balci (2003).

Within the past two decades, many Gülen-inspired businessmen have expanded their businesses globally, especially into the countries of the former Soviet Union and into the Balkans. As they become more financially involved in these countries, they also see the need for better educational opportunities for the youth. It is often these businessmen who initiate plans to build a Gülen school there, pledging their own resources as financial backing and soliciting financial assistance from friends and business associates in Turkey.[11] In the course of interviews, I discovered five businessmen who, on their own, financed the construction and opening of a Gülen school in these countries, including Albania, Bosnia, Turkmenistan, Afghanistan and Pakistan.

The Gülen schools are most numerous in the countries of the former socialist bloc, especially in the former Soviet Union. As former Ottoman provinces the Balkans and central Asian countries were among the first countries to have Gülen schools outside of Turkey. They are also present in Western Europe, especially in the Turkish communities in France, Germany and the Netherlands. Recently, Gulen-inspired schools have opened in both South Asian and African countries.

Outside Turkey the schools have broader cultural and political agendas. In Europe and in the United States, the schools attract Turkish immigrant families who want to raise their children in the "Turkish way." In underdeveloped or developing countries of Africa and Asia, they appeal to students for their quality of teaching, technology and high standards of education. The high concentration of schools in Central Asia appeal to a wide ranging variety of Turkish people, including diaspora Turks and Turkish residents, and serve as a cultural and business center making connections between businessmen, schools and local politicians.[12]

One consequence of the Gülen schools in areas that are actively recruiting youth into terrorist groups is to provide an alternative for the young people. A recent study in southeastern Turkey where the PKK (Kurdistan Workers Party) is very active provides data on several Gülen schools in the area that serve as alternatives for young men who were approached to join the PKK.[13]

Kimse Yok Mu Solidarity and Aid Association (Kimse Yok Mu)

The one exception to the decentralized pattern of initiating and running Gülen-inspired projects is Kimse Yok Mu, the relief organization that evolved into a non-profit charitable organization after the 1999 earthquake in the heart of the Marmara region in Turkey. This Gülen-inspired agency does have a formal, hierarchical structure and organized mechanisms for fundraising.

---

[11] Balci (2003).
[12] Turam (2004).
[13] Kalyoncu (2008).

After 3 years of programming by Samanyolu TV that focused on the needs of the Marmara people and the soliciting of relief funds by the station, in 2002 Kimse Yok Mu Solidarity and Aid Association was established as a foundation. Within several years it expanded its outreach to other people both within Turkey and around the world who need assistance. Contributions of both cash and in-kind donations are collected by the agency. After the earthquake in Pakistan in 2005, $12 million in aid was sent to the region. Similarly, donations were sent to Indonesia after the tsunami disaster in 2004, to Peru after the earthquake and to Ethiopia and Kenya in 2006 to help relieve poverty after the tribal wars there. Currently, Kimse Yok Mu has committed itself to rebuilding an entire township in Darfur, Sudan, over a three year period with a cost of $50 million.

Kimse Yok Mu raises about $16 million annually, some through very creative fundraising techniques. In 2007 donations made directly to an agency bank account amounted to $6.6 million. Approximately $558,000 were donated online with a credit card. Kiosks located in donation boxes on crowded streets and others placed in small business stores collected some $165,000. The most creative technique involved sending text messages to an advertised cell phone number from any of the three major cell phone companies that added the donation amount to the customer's monthly telephone bill. This technique resulted in the raising of almost one million dollars in 2007. The organization also has collection boxes in various locations throughout Istanbul and other cities in Turkey.[14]

Kimse Yok Mu is a nongovernmental agency that was granted "Association of Public Interest" status by the government in 2006. It has corporate headquarters in a five story building in Istanbul, is administered by a President and Chairman of the Executive Committee, collects and distributes cash and in-kind donations from the central headquarters.

Among Kimse Yok Mu's projects are the sister family projects, aid-in-kind, educational aid and foreign aid. In sister family projects the association matches a middle class or wealthy family with a poor family. The better-off family helps the latter with sustenance needs, education and job opportunities. Currently, the association has matched about 1,500 families all over Turkey and plans, over a five year period, to reach over a hundred thousand families.[15]

Through its food bank, Kimse Yok Mu is able to collect food, clothes, hygiene materials and fuel from individuals as well as producers and manufacturers of these products and to distribute them to the needy. In 2007, the association distributed these goods to over two million people in eleven different countries. In addition to these food items, the association collects the meat of sacrificed animals during the Eid of Sacrifice and distributes them to needy people. In 2007, 12,500 sacrificial animals were collected and their meat distributed to 45,000 people in 35 countries as well as to 30,000 people in Turkey.[16]

---

[14] Koc (2008).

[15] Bolukbas (2008).

[16] Ibid.

Kimse Yok Mu also distributes educational equipment and scholarships to needy students in Turkey and elsewhere. The association has provided tutoring services to over 20,000 students with the help of its volunteers. It has also built 11 schools in Pakistan, 4 in Indonesia, 1 in Bangladesh and one in Turkey. After constructing the schools, the association hands them over to the local governments.

The organization also organizes free medical check-ups and medicine to residents in rural areas. Recently Kimse Yok Mu organized local groups of supporters to bring assistance to those in southeast Turkey who are suffering from the PKK conflict there. A group of local doctors examined 8,000 patients in cities and villages there while a group of workers handed out food and clothing that they had acquired from donations in Istanbul, Bursa and other cities in Turkey. More than 50,000 people have benefited from these services, mostly in Turkey but also in some African countries, Pakistan and Bangladesh.

Patterns Within Gülen-Inspired Institutions

There are very clear patterns across the various Gülen-inspired institutions described above, in their origins, their organizational structure, their funding and especially the spirit and culture that permeates them. For these reasons, it is apt to characterize these institutions as Gülen-inspired organizations.

Original Inspiration

In every case, without exception, the inspiration and motivation for the establishment of the institution grew out of the ideas and teachings of Mr. Gülen. The educational projects, including the dormitories, the prep courses and the schools, were the direct results of his constant insistence that education was the answer to the poverty and internal conflicts that he saw within Turkey and also across the world. His burning desire to educate youth was reflected in almost all of his early sermons and writings and can be seen as one of the earliest dreams of Mr. Gülen. He was convinced that educating young people was the answer to the lack of modernization and global recognition of Turkey, as well as the anti-dote to terrorism and conflict in the country and throughout the world.

The media related organizations (i.e. Zaman, Samanyolu TV, the Journalists and Writers Foundation) were founded on the model of objective, balanced and socially responsible reporting that Mr. Gülen advocated, especially in the 1990s. In addition, he insisted that the only way to achieve peace and harmony among diverse groups was to allow free expression of opinions and to create dialog among groups aimed at mutual understanding and respect. All of the media organizations that developed from Mr. Gülen's ideas have these goals as their explicit agenda.

The hospitals were founded in Mr. Gülen's spirit of respect for all people, including patients, and to care for the basic needs of humanity, one of which he saw as adequate and humanitarian medical care. Each Gülen-inspired hospital is dedicated to bringing top-notch medical care not only to those who can afford it but also to patients who need financial assistance to obtain quality medical attention.

Bank Asya is probably the least closely connected to carrying out Mr. Gülen's ideas, even though he agreed in the mid 1990s with some Turkish businessmen that the time had come to provide interest-free banking to those Muslims who refused to put their money into interest-bearing accounts offered by state and private banks in Turkey. While there never were any official ties between Mr. Gülen and Bank Asya, some of the original shareholders in the bank were inspired by Mr. Gülen.

The leadership in Kimse Yok Mu traces the inspiration for the relief agency to Mr. Gülen's concern for needy people wherever they exist. In fact, this is the one institution that I visited that has structured classes and programs for its staff that focus on the ideas of Mr. Gülen as a source of inspiration.

While the teachings of Mr. Gülen is the inspiration behind all of the Gülen projects and the fact that he was initially involved in some of them such as the first dormitories and prep courses, as well as his attendance at the opening of Bank Asya, he remains involved on a day to day basis in very few of them. The sole exceptions are the fact that he writes a weekly column for Zaman newspaper and has many of his books published by the Journalists and Writers Foundation. He has no ongoing ties with Bank Asya, Samanyolu TV, Fatih University, the hospitals, the schools, or the relief organization. There is a pattern for groups of businessmen to travel to the United States where Mr. Gülen now lives, to consult with him as they plan a project or when a specific issue arises for which they seek advice. For example, he was consulted as plans for Bank Asya were being made and recently by administrators at Fatih University when they were invited to apply for a development grant from the Turkish government underwritten by Saudi Arabia to finance expansion of the university. Gülen recommended that they rely solely on Turkish sources. Other than these periodic and very specific occasions, Mr. Gülen is not involved in the daily operations of the institutions inspired by his ideas.

Permeating Ideas

There is an organizational culture in each of the Gülen institutions that I visited, created by the Gülen-inspired ideas and ideals that permeate them. These ideals are so strong and pervasive that they mark the organizations with common characteristics. These include the following: educating the youth in society to combine spirituality with intellectual training; providing modern education in all areas of life; emphasizing Turkish nationalism and an appreciation of the Turkish past; engaging in intercultural and interfaith dialog; tolerance of different ideas and opinions; love and respect for all humanity; a global perspective; hospitality; and giving service and help to one's fellow human beings.

Whether in the educational settings, the hospitals, the relief organization or the media settings, the above qualities were evident in the ways in which the organizations were structured, their goals and in the personnel who staffed the institutions. How is it achieved? The fact that a core group in each of the organizations consists of participants in the Gülen movement, most of whom are part of local circles within their professions and neighborhoods, means that these people consistently study and discuss the teachings and writings of Mr. Gülen as well as the entire Islamic prophetic tradition. There is a cadre of personnel, therefore, who are socialized into a common set of ideas and values. In addition, while being a member of the movement is not a requirement for employment in the schools, dormitories, hospitals or at Kimse Yok Mu, careful attention is given to hiring only those people who share the same values and goals as the core group of movement members. Through these mechanisms of socialization and hiring, therefore, a culture is created that marks each of the institutions as Gülen-inspired.

Commitment of Personnel

In addition to sharing a common culture of ideas and values, and as part of this culture, a major reason for the success of the Gülen institutions is the commitment and dedication of the personnel who run them. Whether I interviewed doctors or administrators in the hospitals, principals or teachers in the schools, the vice-rector at Fatih University, or the staff at Kimse Yok Mu, all of them commented that they were working there not just to earn a salary but because they believed in what they were doing. As a result, work days tended to extend beyond a normal eight hour day, staff took on responsibility and care for patients and students beyond the usual demands of the job and complaints and job dissatisfaction were minimal. Rather, throughout the institutions the people I met and interviewed were very happy to be there, felt they were part of worthwhile activities and were grateful that they could serve their fellowman. In addition to these idealistic motivations, it is also the case that being part of a Gülen-inspired school or project also provided strong social support and a meaningful community. Also, for example, teachers in the schools were guaranteed that they and their families would be taken care of in terms of job security, housing and medical expenses. All of these rewards provided motivation for the personnel to be committed to their jobs and relieved them of many of the worries that plague many workers.

Financial Support

With the exception of Bank Asya which was a business venture from the beginning, the remaining Gülen-inspired projects were all originally financed by groups of local supporters who wanted to make Mr. Gülen's ideas reality by creating institutions with organizational cultures that would express these ideals. Characteristic of the Gülen movement is its decentralized, local organization. In every case I studied, the initiation, planning and financing of the schools, dormitories, prep courses, hospitals and media organizations began when a group of Gülen supporters, usually including local businessmen, came together and decided that there was a need in their community for a specific institution. They then pledged their own money and in-kind donations and solicited financial assistance from family, friends and acquaintances. In most instances they established a foundation or business to collect and administer the project or projects in their particular locale.

As Gülen schools were introduced into countries outside of Turkey, especially those in the former countries of the Soviet Union, the usual pattern was for one or several Turkish businessmen who had operations in the particular country to initiate and finance a local school, often with financial support from business acquaintances in Turkey. In many instances, one or several local Gülen circles of supporters adopt a school in another country and offer financial support for that school. In other instances, a businessman in Turkey will agree to build and maintain a school abroad. I heard many examples of Gülen supporters in Turkey who visited their sister-schools and expressed great pride in the school.

The usual pattern in all of the Gülen-inspired institutions is that they rely on sponsor support for the original buildings and operation of the institution. However, in all instances these projects became self supporting within a few years. Most of the schools I visited were able to provide their own support through tuition and fees within 2–3 years of their opening. All of the schools provide scholarships for some financially needy students who cannot afford the tuition which ranges from $5,000–9,000 per year. In most instances, local supporters continue to provide some of these scholarships. Other than that, however, the schools become self-supporting institutions and do not require financial support beyond their initial few years. The usual pattern, as I saw in Bursa, was for the original group of supporters to find a new project once the original school no longer required their financial support. In Bursa there are now six Gülen-inspired schools and the seventh will open shortly, all of them being financed by local supporters in the Gülen movement. Likewise, both Sema Hospital in Istanbul and Bahar Hospital in Bursa are now self supportive, even though they relied on sponsor support to get started and to operate in their early years.

Quality Institutions

A major characteristic of the Gülen institutions is their recognized quality, regardless of the sector in which they are operating. The Gülen-inspired schools are recognized both in Turkey and in many of the other countries in which they now operate as first-rate schools. The fact that a very high percentage of their students pass the university entrance exam and go to colleges within Turkey and abroad and the extraordinary number of students from Gülen schools who win top prizes in the Turkish as well as national academic Olympiads is testimony to the excellence of the education provided in these schools.

The hospitals associated with the movement likewise have a reputation in Turkey of being among the best of the private hospitals. Because physician salaries are competitive for private hospitals and because of the patient-oriented care that characterizes these medical institutions, some of the best doctors in Turkey gravitate there. Both Sema and Bahar hospitals had state-of-art equipment, such as digital magnetic resonating machines in their laboratories and the ability to perform open heart surgeries with the latest equipment. For some of this equipment, local supporters continue to provide financial assistance so that the hospitals can buy the latest and most advanced equipment on the medical market.

Bank Asya is now the largest of the participation banks in Turkey. Even though it obtained the most recent participation bank license offered by the government, within 12 years it has garnered one third of the market for such banks in Turkey with current deposits of $5 billion. Likewise, Zaman newspaper now has the largest circulation of any newspaper in Turkey. The Journalists and Writers Foundation, although only 14 years old, has been able to bring together religious and political leaders for interfaith and intercultural dialog from many arenas of conflict in Turkey and around the world. For example, in 2006, leaders from the major religious groups in Turkey (e.g. Muslims, Christian Orthodox, Jews) were brought together in Göteborg, Sweden, to discuss issues that both divide and unite the communities. That same year the Foundation sponsored a dialog between Turkish and French leaders to discuss cultural pluralism in Europe. It has held a number of meetings to discuss Turkish membership in the European Union, including one in Egypt in 2007, that focused on Islam, the West and Modernization. The Foundation has been recognized by many governments and non-governmental organizations, including the government of Turkmenistan, the Russian Federation Association and Hartford Seminary in the United States, for being among the most effective in creating dialog among groups long in conflict with one another.

Therefore, regardless of the sector in which they operate, Gülen-inspired institutions share the above characteristics which mark these endeavors as first rate, quality institutions. This occurs in large part because of the commitment of the volunteers and supporters who give of their time, talents and financial resources to bring about the kinds of service projects strongly advocated by Gülen in order to create a better society wherever they are located.

Summary

I began the research described in this book with three basic questions: what are the organizational mechanisms that generate commitment and enthusiasm on the part of movement supporters and that help explain why the Gülen movement is spreading as a transnational movement? How does member commitment relate to the financial mechanisms that support service projects in ways that promote the involvement, enthusiasm and commitment of movement supporters? What are the financial arrangements related to the institutions associated with the movement and in what ways are supporters related financially to Gülen-inspired projects? In this final chapter I summarize responses to these three issues based on the interviews that I conducted with a wide array of supporters of the Gülen movement, both in Turkey and in Houston, Texas.

In order to address the above research questions, I conducted both individual and focus group interviews with business owners, professionals and blue collar workers in cities, towns and villages in Turkey (e.g. Istanbul, Ankara, Bursa, Keyseri and Mudanya). In addition, I interviewed supporters of a local group in Houston, Texas. Included were both men and women of varying socio-economic backgrounds and length of time of involvement with the movement. In addition, I interviewed CEOs, principals of schools and major administrative officers in the following Gülen-inspired institutions: Bank Asya, Samanyolu television station, Zaman newspaper, the Journalists and Writers Foundation, Fatih University, Sema and Bahar Hospitals, five Gülen-inspired schools and Kimse Yok Mu Solidarity and Aid Association.

As part of the original project to answer the questions outlined above, I interviewed only members in the movement. Methodologically, to determine what motivates people to be committed to an organization and to ascertain the mechanisms of financing within specific institutions, it makes sense to ask those involved in the organizations. As a result, this book is **NOT** a critical evaluation of the movement from various perspectives. To achieve such a goal would require a different methodology, including interviewing people with different perspectives on the movement. Rather, the book is a sociological analysis of the structure of the movement, with emphasis upon mechanisms of membership commitment and the service projects that are outcomes of the movement.

H.R. Ebaugh, *The Gülen Movement: A Sociological Analysis of a Civic Movement Rooted in Moderate Islam*, DOI 10.1007/978-1-4020-9894-9_7,
© Springer Science+Business Media B.V. 2010

Given my academic training as a sociologist, it is the sociological perspective that provides the lens with which I formulated the research design. Given the voluntary nature of participation in the movement and the non-hierarchical structure that was apparent, I was especially focused on the structural and motivational mechanisms that promoted commitment to the goals and projects of the movement. Given the fact that hundreds of top-notch schools were somehow related to the movement, as well as six private hospitals, a media empire, a private university and a disaster relief agency, I realized that the issue of finances must be addressed as part of the organizational analysis. I also suspected, from the beginning, based on traditional organizational theory, that a strong relationship exists between financial structures and membership commitment.

In conversations with colleagues, students and a number of potential publishers, I realized that few Western readers had even heard of Fethullah Gülen or the Gülen movement. It was necessary, therefore, to begin with a chapter on the life and teachings of Mr. Gülen as well as a brief history of the movement that he inspired. In addition, the movement is very definitely Turkish, not only given the fact that the majority of supporters are Turkish, but especially in terms of its historical and political origins. I doubt that the Gülen movement could have arisen in its specific form and focus in any other country in the world. Its roots lie in the particular historical period that existed some four decades after the birth of the Turkish Republic. The evolution of the movement was highly influenced by social and political events that unfolded in Turkey during the 1960s and the ensuing four decades, as well as events that have occurred since the turn of the new 21st century. I felt compelled, therefore, to include a brief chapter on the history of Turkey, with special focus on the relationships between Islam and the state.

Research Findings

I now turn now to the three research questions that have guided the data and organization of this book and briefly summarize my findings.

1. **What are the organizational commitment mechanisms that attract and maintain members in the movement?** From the sociological perspective of organizational theory, especially those theories that predict membership commitment and resource mobilization, the basic structural aspect of the movement that generates commitment lies within the local circles. These circles consist of businessmen, professionals and workers in Turkish cities, towns and rural areas who meet regularly to read Qur'anic commentary and Muslim scholars, especially Mr. Gülen, to pray together, to share ideas and needs of people in the group and to determine service projects (e.g. schools, hospitals, student dorms, disaster relief, etc.) that the group chooses to support financially. Oftentimes, the local circles consist of people who are in the same profession (e.g. doctors, lawyers,

businessmen, factory workers) or who live in the same residential community. These natural groupings promote friendship as well as networks that facilitate professional and business relationships.

The local circles are based on the traditional Turkish *cemaat*, a type of grassroots social group that evolved after the formation of the Republic and the outlawing of the Sufi orders and *madrasas*. *Cemaats* were formed by practicing Muslims who wanted to preserve the Islamic heritage while adapting to modernity. They were organized around scholars and intellectuals who blended religious devotion with a form of nationalism or individualized spiritual practices.

Mr. Gülen, as a young man, was part of a *cemaat* organized around the teachings of Said Nursi, a Sufi scholar who promoted harmony between science and reason, on the one hand, and revelation and faith on the other. As Mr. Gülen's ideas began to attract supporters in Turkey in the late 1960s and early 1970s, he encouraged those interested to join together in *cemaats* to discuss his ideas as they related to contemporary Turkish society.

My interviews with members in the Gülen movement demonstrate clearly that the social ties provided by being part of a local circle are a major reward for members. Overwhelmingly, movement supporters described their membership in a local circle as a major defining element in their lives and one that permeates their identity, priorities and daily lives.

The Gülen movement has no formally organized, hierarchical structure but is, rather, a loosely coordinated network of local circles, each having its own autonomy in terms of content and frequency of meetings, diversity of members and projects to be supported. This grassroots structure promotes commitment and involvement since nothing gets done that is not initiated and carried out by the members. The decentralized authority and administrative structure promotes member involvement and a sense of responsibility on the part of the millions of participants who have a personal stake in the achievements of the movement. The result is a highly cohesive group that shares the goals and vision put forth by Fethullah Gülen and a commitment to one another as well as projects decided upon by the group.

2. **In what ways do the financial mechanisms involved in funding the service projects promote the involvement, enthusiasm and commitment of movement supporters? How are supporters motivated to donate?** Financial giving is an inherent element among supporters in the Gülen movement. Mr. Gülen repeatedly, in his sermons and writings over the years, encourages supporters to give in whatever ways they are able, including service in the schools, hospitals and relief agencies as well as financial support for the service projects. As a result, many supporters, especially in the early years of the movement, attended schools of education and became administrators and teachers in the Gülen-inspired schools and sacrificed more lucrative careers in order to have a part in creating the kinds of quality schools that Mr. Gülen envisioned for Turkey.

Mr. Gülen preached that everyone had a part to play in bringing about his vision for improved education for every youth in Turkey. He constantly encouraged wealthy entrepreneurs and small businessmen, alike, to support quality education and to establish trusts to support grade and high schools, dormitories, and preparatory schools to prepare high school students for the mandatory university exam. To be able to provide such donations, he encouraged supporters to grow their businesses as much as possible, especially globally, which he saw as the economic future of the world. A portion of the accumulated wealth, therefore, should be used to support educational projects that would eliminate ignorance, poverty and immorality among the youth. Mr. Gülen argued that a strong free market is necessary to produce economic wealth which can support a modern educational system.

In encouraging an ethos of giving, Mr. Gülen called upon a long tradition in Turkish, Islamic culture. In addition to *zakat*, one of the five pillars of Islam, that requires the payment of a certain portion of one's wealth to the poor once a year, *sadaka* is a charitable gift which is given with the sole intention of pleasing God and in expectation of a reward in the Hereafter. The notion of neighborliness or hospitality (*komsuluk*) is entrenched in Turkish culture and is traced to words and actions of the Prophet who emphasized the importance of good relations with neighbors. In requesting that people support quality schools and educational projects in whatever ways they were able, Mr. Gülen expressed his call to action in terms of these fundamental Turkish–Islamic values. He simply provided ways in which they could express the generosity and giving that are embedded in their culture and religion.

Repeatedly, interviewees stated that everyone involved in the movement makes some kind of financial contribution depending on his/her circumstances. There was widespread agreement among people in the various local circles that donations vary between 5% and 20% with 10% of yearly income as an average. A small group of businessmen make contributions over 20%, including some that divide their yearly profits into thirds, with one third going back into the business, one third used as living expenses and one third donated to the movement to support one or more service projects.

An unanticipated consequence of financial giving on the part of virtually every supporter in the movement is the generation of commitment to the group, its basic teachings and ideals, and the projects which it supports. A major strength of the local circles is the constant discussion of concepts of giving in the Qur'an, the prophetic tradition and the works of Mr. Gülen. These circles, therefore, provide the spiritual motivation for giving and define donations as an integral part of one's religious and patriotic lives. In addition to defining projects worthy of support, the financial giving not only demonstrates commitment to the movement and its good works but generates such commitment by creating a sense of mutual ownership of the service projects.

3. **What are the financial arrangements related to the institutions that are associated with the Gülen movement and in what ways are supporters related financially to Gülen-inspired projects?** First and foremost, Mr. Gülen has never had personal wealth to sponsor projects so it is clear that it never has been nor is it today his own money that is behind the many projects that he initially inspires and that are administered by his supporters. In his earlier years, he appeared at many fund-raising events and visited wealthy individuals to try to

convince them to support excellent schools and educational projects in the country. However, apart from motivating people to make financial contributions to projects, he has maintained his distance from all financial involvements and encourages local groups to both raise money for local projects and to oversee their operations. This approach has built trust and confidence in his intentions.

With the exception of Bank Asya which was a business venture from the beginning, the remaining Gülen-inspired projects that I studied were all financed primarily by groups of local supporters. Given the decentralized, local organization of the movement, in every case the initiation, planning and financing of the projects began when a group of Gülen supporters, usually including local businessmen, came together and decided that there was a need in the community for a specific institution. They then pledged their own money and solicited others in the community to step forward and contribute, usually through a foundation or business that would collect and administer the project (s).

The usual pattern in Gülen-inspired institutions is that they rely on sponsor support for the original buildings and operation of the institution. However, within a few years these projects become self-supporting through tuition, fees, subscriptions, client payments, etc. As a school or hospital becomes financially independent of sponsor support, the pattern is for sponsors to build a new school or hospital in an area where such a need exists, either within Turkey or in another country.

In the 1990s, first in those former countries of the Soviet Union, the pattern was for one or several Turkish businessmen who had business ties in the particular country to gather together local community leaders and business leaders and to encourage them to determine needs in their local areas. The businessmen would then initiate and finance a local project, usually a school, often with support from fellow businessmen in Turkey. Over time, as the schools became self-supportive, the businessmen became less involved and turned over the school to local support and administration.

In summary, the Gülen movement is a loosely organized network of local organizations whose supporters interact through meeting in local circles. Within these circles, supporters read and discuss ideas gleaned from the Qur'an and Islamic scholars, especially Futhullah Gülen. In addition, the local group supports one another both emotionally and by material assistance when necessary. The group also selects Gülen-inspired projects such as schools, preparatory courses, dormitories, hospitals and relief efforts which it decides to support through voluntary work and financial contributions. Involvement in the local circles, along with financial donations, generate the type of commitment to the movement that has resulted in its spread to over 100 countries on five continents.

In conclusion, the Gülen movement is a civic initiative first begun in Turkey in the 1960s by Mr. Fethullah Gülen and currently spreading worldwide via the Turkish diaspora. The movement advocates quality, modern education for all youth, interfaith and intercultural dialog, and mutual cooperation among cultural and religious groups. These basic goals of the movement, along with the contributions of its numerous service projects, has resulted in the recognition of the Gülen movement as an important player in promoting peaceful coexistence and global peace.

Appendix: Voices of the Critics

During field trips to Turkey and in conversations with Turkish immigrants in Houston, it became clear that the Gülen movement has its critics. In an effort to learn the nature of these criticisms, we conducted 25 interviews with a wide array of vocal critics, including university professors, journalists, businessmen, graduate students, retired military personnel, lawyers and working people who were identified as having strong views regarding the movement. This data is reported in an appendix rather than in the body of the book because my original research design did not include interviews with critics of the movement. It was only in the course of writing of the book that I had the opportunity to interview some of the critics. I did not conduct a random sample of critics and, no doubt, talked to the most outspoken and vocal among them.

The purpose of this appendix is to indicate that the Gülen movement is controversial, both in Turkey and in the Turkish Diaspora, and to indicate some of the major concerns that the critics have in regard to the movement. I will present the major criticisms mentioned in our interviews and then describe data presented in this book from interviews with members in the movement, as well as statements of Mr. Gülen, that address the criticisms. The appendix, in no way, is intended as an evaluation of the movement; rather, my intent is to indicate the fact that not all Turks are movement supporters and that strong objections to the movement exist.

Fear of an Islamic State

First and most often repeated is the fear that Mr. Gülen is building a strong base of supporters in order to overturn the "secularism" introduced into Turkey by Ataturk. As discussed in Chapter 2, "Islam and the State Throughout Turkish History", on October 29, 1923, Ataturk proposed an amendment in Parliament that transformed the nation into "the Republic of Turkey" and abolished the caliphate, the Ministry of Religious Endowments and the office of the highest religious authority in the country. Parliament closed the *sharia* courts, shut down *madrasas*, placed all religious organizations under government control, repealed Islamic Law, and substituted a new penal code. A few years later, in 1928, Parliament deleted the phrase "the religion of the Turkish state is Islam" from the Constitution and in 1937 the Constitution was amended to state that Turkey was, indeed, a secular state. Thus, the potential for an Islamic state was crippled in favor of the legitimacy of the Republican, secularist regime.[1] Ataturk believed that Turkey must leave its Ottoman past behind and follow the example of progress and modernization set by Europe and the Western world. For over 70 years, the Republic of Turkey has been governed as a secularist state, with religion strictly allocated to the private sphere, modeled after the system of laicization that Ataturk and the other young Turks adapted from the French. Mr. Gülen's critics are afraid that his intentions are to reverse the secular republic inspired by Ataturk and to create an Islamic state in Turkey like that brought to Iran by the Ayatollah Khomeini in 1979. They fear that the movement is a calculated threat against the secular government in Turkey and that Mr. Gülen and his supporters are laying the groundwork in terms of large numbers of followers and substantial financial resources with the intention of overtaking the Turkish government at some point in the future.

Having read hundreds of pages of Mr. Gülen's speeches and writings, and having talked to over a hundred of his followers, I see no evidence that he intends to take over the Turkish state and replace the secular government with an Islamic state. In fact, Mr. Gülen shies away from political discussions. Likewise, his followers seldom engage in political discussions, do not organize grassroots political action groups and are not focused on changing the political structure either in Turkey or in the countries where they are located. Based on my data, I agree with Graham Fuller, the former vice chairman of the National Intelligence Council at the CIA, that the Gülen movement is not a political movement but rather a social movement that aims to change the hearts and minds of individuals in the direction of greater tolerance, social responsibility and modernization in terms of educational and scientific achievements.

Gülen and his supporters do not challenge the reforms introduced by Ataturk in terms of modernization, a stronger Turkey and the importance of education and advancement in scientific achievements. Rather, the movement is very much a nationalist one in terms of devotion and loyalty to the nation. The argument of Mr. Gülen is that scientific advancement and modernization can take place along with commitment to Islamic ideals and identity as a practicing Muslim.

Repeatedly, what I heard in the interviews with members in the movement was the advocacy of greater freedom to practice one's religion in public places rather than strict control of religious institutions and behaviors by the state. The comparison was frequently made between the Turkish system of *laicite* (described in detail in Chapter 2) based on state control of religion and emphasizing the absence of religious practice in public spaces, and the system of the separation of church and state that is law in the United States. In the U.S. system, religion and politics are seen as two separate spheres. Religious organizations as well as individuals have great

---

[1] Cetin (2008).

latitude to practice their beliefs and rituals without the interference of the state. Likewise, religious organizations have limitations in regard to influencing state affairs. Americans are free, except in rare instances,[2] to wear distinctively religious attire in public and to exercise their religious freedoms. Gülen supporters frequently commented that they want greater freedom to practice their religion publicly without the interference of the state.

In regard to the subtle strategy of Gülen followers "infiltrating" top government, military, policy and other civil services in a slow and systematic plan to eventually take over these agencies, it is logical that some Gülen followers would be in these agencies, given the fact that it is estimated that approximately 8–10% of the Turkish population is connected to the movement in some way or other. Based on statistical probability alone, given a total population of 70 million, and the fact that many Gülen followers are well educated, it makes sense that some proportion of the 5.6–7 million people would have jobs in these sectors. Nowhere in my data, however, did I discover evidence of a systematic plan to place followers in these agencies in order to eventually achieve a take-over.

There is evidence that some political parties in Turkey are more sympathetic to Mr. Gülen and his followers than others and that the political context of Turkey impacts the growth and activities of the movement both in Turkey and abroad. There is also evidence that Mr. Gülen advocates that those inspired by his ideas be part of all institutions in society, including government agencies and the military, rather than retreat to Qur'anic schools and isolated sectors of the society. However, I see no concrete evidence to support the contention that either Mr. Gülen or those who are inspired by him are systematically or deliberately placing people in top government and military positions with the intention of a gradual coup or take-over.

Gülen as an Agent of the U.S. Government

The second major fear expressed by the critics whom we interviewed is that Mr. Gülen and his many service projects are being financed by the United States, especially the Central Intelligence Agency (CIA). One frequently mentioned reason for this contention is that the movement generates billions of dollars and that such large sums must come from some governmental source. Also is the contention that the United States is supporting Mr. Gülen and his movement because it represents moderate Islam and it is the hope of the West that such a version of Islam will dominate the region and be an antidote to terrorism and radical Islam.

---

[2] Exceptions relate to issues of security such as restrictions placed on the Sikhs regarding the carrying of metal swords or daggers through metal detectors or freedom to wear the turban in specific army situations. The Yoruba and Native Americans are required to obtain special permission to slaughter certain animals or to use peyote in their religious ceremonies.

In regard to the movement being financially supported by some government, including the U.S. Central Intelligence Agency, I find no empirical evidence to support this contention. There are several pieces of data that challenge the supposition put forth by the critics. First, over the past several decades, Mr. Gülen and the organizations associated with him and his movement have been vetted and reviewed by numerous governmental agencies such as the Turkish Department of the Treasury and the state prosecutor's office. Every year the Treasury Department reviews the financial books of both for profit and nonprofit businesses. Thus, Bank Asya, Zaman newspaper, Samanyolu t.v. and the Journalists and Writers Foundation are required to open their financial books to government inspectors. Not once, as far as I can determine, were any suspicious funds discovered or unaccounted for. Likewise, no financial transgressions were discovered that would arouse the suspicion that foreign governments were funding the operations.

Likewise, for six years a legal case against Mr. Gülen was pending in the Turkish courts. Civil lawyers poured over documents of all kinds in an attempt to bring evidence of wrongdoing or suspicious activities against Mr. Gülen and his movement. In June, 2007, the case was finally dismissed on the basis of lack of evidence. If there were foreign governments involved in the finances of the movement, I am convinced that such ties would have been exposed by government regulators or lawyers.

In the recent case of Mr. Gülen's application for a green card in the U.S. (June 2008), a lawyer for the prosecution quoted a paper given my myself and Dogan Koc at the London School of Economics in fall, 2007. In an attempt to deny the request, the lawyer referred to our paper as indicating that the CIA might be behind the funding of the movement when, in fact, we say explicitly that **opponents** of the movement claim that the CIA may be financially supporting the movement.

The argument that such large sums of money are involved in the support of service projects that some government must be involved falls short in the light of the amounts of money contributed by wealthy businessmen in Turkey as well as the large donor base in the movement. As shown in Chapters "The Network of Local Circles" and "The Water for the Mill: Financing of Gülen-Inspired Service Projects", many very wealthy businessmen contribute 10–50% of their yearly income to the movement projects, with many donating one-third to the movement. If one considers an annual income of millions of dollars on the part of hundreds of these businessmen, the contributions add up quickly. In addition to monetary contributions, both the donation of property and construction materials as well as labor-time, point to a financially successful movement.

In addition to the large contributions from wealthy businessmen, millions of members in the movement contribute smaller amounts of money, materials, services and labor time. My data show that the average contribution is about 10% of yearly income regardless of occupation and status. Multiplied by 8–10 million participants worldwide in the movement, the amount of donations is no small sum. The argument that there must be a government entity involved because of the billions of dollars involved is hollow in the light of these data.

Brainwashing of Poor, Illiterate People

A third fear that was frequently expressed was that Mr. Gülen as well as his followers were taking advantage of uneducated, rural people in Turkey, especially young people, luring them into dormitories and light houses associated with the movement, offering them scholarships and opportunities, and then brainwashing them with ideas inherent in the movement. A female member of the Turkish Women's Union said, "These Gülen people aid poor families and take successful students from their homes. They don't know what kind of education they get in their private teaching institutions. They brainwash these children and educate them for themselves. These people are not patriots but religious."

A hotel manager who is critical of the movement reiterated similar ideas: "They select potentially bright students and educate them to get stronger. It is even better for them when these people are poor. In this way they can control them easily. They don't invest for free. They have expectations in return."

The issue of "brainwashing" poor, illiterate people is basically an ideological one. As was very evident in the spate of articles in the 1980s regarding issues of brainwashing in the new religious movements (NRMs) or "cults" as they were commonly known, the term "brainwashing" has ideological overtones.[3] What is brainwashing to opponents of an idea is often spirituality or opportunity for proponents. As I listened to dozens of blue collar workers in local circles in Turkey, what I heard was gratitude to the movement for the opportunities provided them and their siblings and friends to escape rural poverty and poor educational systems in exchange for scholarships to prep courses, university, medical and law school, and the chance to live in the dormitories. In addition to career opportunities, these workers were also grateful to be part of a social group that meets regularly, helps one another and provides opportunity for other poor students.

Taking Turkey Backwards in Its Move Toward Modernization

There is the fear that some of Mr. Gülen's ideas are a return to traditional customs and values that are not compatible with modernization, scientific development and democracy. In particular, as one politician commented, "I met Gülen personally. He is a person who does not shake hands with women. He does not even look them in the face. He gives sermons and cries all the time. He is an obvious pawn. He is uneducated, but an effective preacher." A male journalist said, "There cannot be any positive consequences in the movement because they want to take us back to the period before the Republic was established. We should target reasoning and questioning but they stress dogma that is not scientific. They try to create a country ruled by imams and devotees. They want to live in such a society."

---

[3] Barker (1984); Robbins and Anthony (1990); Bromley and Richardson (1984).

The issue of limiting the rights of women and encouraging the headscarf for women were fears expressed by over half of the 25 interviewees and by all seven of the women. For example, a female professor said, "They want moderate Islam in Turkey...In moderate Islam men and women are separated. Women work at home like in my grandmother's generation. Men and women should be equal in every aspect of life such as career and promotions. Women can be both mothers and professionals at the same time... If women are less educated, exposed to violence and under pressure in a male dominated country, there cannot be freedom. The culture of religious orders avoids freedom because they are oppressive."

In regard to the Gülen movement taking Turkey backwards in terms of modernization and scientific development, both the speeches and writings of Mr. Gülen as well as what is being achieved in the schools and hospitals associated with him point in exactly the opposite direction. Repeatedly, he encourages his followers to obtain the best and most advanced education they can, especially in the sciences, in order to contribute to the modernization of Turkey. In the schools I visited I was amazed at the modern scientific labs in which students were learning, as well as the many trophies displayed in the lobbies of students who had competed successfully in the international science Olympiads. There is no doubt that the Gülen-inspired schools are providing among the best and most modern education available in Turkey today and that many people who can afford it are sending their children to these schools, whether they are in the movement or not.

Likewise, in the three hospitals I visited associated with the movement was state-of-the-art laboratory equipment and among the best trained doctors in the country. For example, in Bahar Hospital in Bursa is a top rated optomology clinic, a cardiac unit capable of performing open heart surgery and a laser machine that can perform colonoscopies noninvasively. In terms of science and technological modernization, the Gülen-affiliated institutions are in the forefront of moving Turkey into the modern, competitive world.

The one area that is problematic in terms of the lack of modernization in the movement, in my opinion, are attitudes toward the role of women in the world. Emphasizing wearing of the headscarf is minor and basically a matter of personal preference.[4] More importantly, in some areas such as Houston, women are seldom public figures in the movement, either in key positions, public events or within the institutions financed by the movement. Women tend to be in the background performing the traditional tasks of childcare, housekeeping, cooking, teaching in the schools and mosques, and deferring to their husbands in public arenas. In part, the role of women may be dictated by Turkish culture and the fact that many women outside of Turkey have followed their husbands to jobs and universities as students and are uncomfortable with non-Turkish languages. However, as the movement becomes more worldwide and becomes less Turkish, a major challenge in its goal of modernization and adaptation to other cultures is dealing with the role of women in the movement and in the broader culture. This challenge is confounded

---

[4] For discussions of the veil, see Read (2004); (2000).

by contradictory remarks of Mr. Gülen who says repeatedly that women are very important because they are the primary caretakers and socializing agents of the young children. This is a very traditional statement that values women because of their role as mothers and homemakers rather than acknowledging the dual responsibility of men and women in the raising of children. As the movement spreads to modern, industrialized countries it will be faced with the challenge of redefining the role of women.

The Gülen Movement Supports Only Its Own People

About one fourth of the interviewees accused the movement of discrimination by providing resources such as scholarships and educational opportunity to its supporters, while neglecting other needy people in Turkish society. A Turkish professor said, "They are trying to separate the country. There is no tolerance for people that are not one of them. Fethullah followers exclude others. They give scholarships, establish schools and give food to their own followers. These are not for humanitarian purposes but they are all planned." A businessmen who does business with Fethullah followers commented, "They told us that they help students that are in need. They support the ones that are one of them."

The accusation that the movement supports only its own members and is discriminatory toward other needy people in the society is totally unsubstantiated by my data. In all the schools I visited, less than half of the students are affiliated with the movement. Many parents send their children to the schools because of their outstanding academic reputation. In addition, each school provides scholarships to needy students who qualify in terms of grades but whose families cannot afford the tuition. In most of these schools, about 20% of the student body is there on scholarship and many of those qualifying for need based aid are not children of movement members. Likewise, a proportion of the students in the dormitories are supported by scholarships and these recipients are not necessarily children of people in the movement. Many of the workers I interviewed said that they would like their children to go to Gülen-inspired schools or to live in the dormitories but that they are not able to get their children into these institutions. Therefore, the contention that the movement supports only its own is not rooted in data.

Within the past several years there have been hundreds of movement followers who have gone to southeastern Turkey to assist the needy people there who are suffering because of the recent PKK conflict in the area. Thousands of pounds of meat and other foodstuffs, as well as clothing and money, were collected and taken to the area to help those in need. The recipients of these gifts were not only participants in the movement but the needy, whomever they are. Likewise, teams of doctors have gone to the area to assess the medical needs and to transport sick patients to Gülen hospitals in both Istanbul and Bursa. Again, as far as I could tell, no one asked whether or not the poor and needy people were members of the Gülen movement. The victims who were assisted after the 2004 earthquake in the Mardin region were not only Gülen supporters. So the accusation that the movement helps only its own people is not substantiated by data.

The Movement as a Secret Society or Sect

There is fear that Mr. Gülen and those who follow him have plans and goals that they are not making public. Critics contend that what is said publicly by the movement members is not the whole story but that there are clandestine activities going on with the purpose of taking over the Turkish government and society. For example, a professor said, "I am not an enemy of Fethullah followers. They are good people. What frightens me are their intentions, because it is secret. I can't see their purpose. I am sure that it is a systematic plan."

The fact that people associated with the Gülen movement, including top officers of Bank Asya, Zaman newspaper, Samanyolu T.V. station and the Journalists and Writers Foundation, as well as leading businessmen in Istanbul and Bursa, and groups of professional and blue collar workers alike were willing and eager to talk with me about finances in the movement demonstrates to me that the movement is not as "secretive" as its critics claim. Mr. Gülen, himself, has said several times recently that it is very important for the movement to be financially transparent. In fact, in the case of the bank, the newspaper and the TV station, the financial statements are public and available on the internet. The speeches and articles of Mr. Gülen are accessible via a website. The accusation of "secretiveness" seems, to me, based more on imagination of clandestine activities than on empirical data that points to goals and involvements that are not made public.

In summary, therefore, I am respectful of the fears expressed by the Kemalists that Turkey's history of secularism might be threatened and overthrown by an authoritarian leader with a strong following and replaced with the type of Islamic state that exists in Iran. However, the critics present no empirical data relating their fears to actual events and behaviors associated with Mr. Gülen or members of his movement. Likewise, the empirical data (e.g. interviews, field visits, review of records and documents) that I gathered over the past 12 months related to the Gülen movement do not substantiate the accusations and fears expressed by critics of the movement.

Further Evidence

In addition to the data presented in the previous section that raise challenges regarding the apprehensions of the critics toward the Gülen movement, key characteristics of the group do not fit the model that describes sectarian groups whose aim is to challenge the status quo in society and to promote its own agenda. These characteristics are: absence of visibility and transparency; isolation; authoritarian control;

traditionalism as opposed to modernization; and use of violence to achieve group goals.[5] The Gülen movement does not display the above qualities that would make it more likely to evolve into a political group whose goal is to infiltrate and over-throw the existing regime in society. The following descriptions of the movement demonstrate this point.

Integration Into Society (as Opposed to Isolation)

Sectarian groups whose goal is either to challenge the existing social structures of society (e.g. the Branch Davidians;[6] Christian Identity Movement;[7] Aum Shinrikyo[8]) or to create an alternative society of their own (e.g. Amish;[9] Fundamentalist Latter Day Saints;[10] Unification Church[11]) tend to be isolationist, that is, to remove them-selves residentially, socially and politically from mainstream society. The Gülen movement has never had as its goal to create a unique sect or unit within Islam or Turkey. Neither is it a dissenting faction aggregated around a common interest, belief or utopia. It is not required that members or supporters of the movement live apart from others in society. Rather, movement members are encouraged to dialog and interact with their fellow citizens of all creeds, races and socio-economic backgrounds.

Continuously, Mr. Gülen reminds people of the current interdependency of communities and that any meaningful change in a country will not be determined by that country alone because this is a period of interactive relations, a situation that causes closeness between peoples and nations. He argues that differences in beliefs, races, customs and traditions create richness in the world, and should be appreciated for the common good through peaceful and respectful relationships.[12] This does not mean diluting beliefs and practices but respecting those of others while affirming one's own commitments. In Gülen's words:

> We should know how to be ourselves and then remain ourselves. That does not mean isolation from others. It means preservation of our essential identity among others, following our way among other ways. While self-identity is necessary, we should also find the ways to a universal integration. Isolation from the world will eventually result in annihilation.[13]

---

[5] For examples of such groups see Juergensmeyer (2000); Zeskind (1986); Sprinzak (1991); Reader (1996); Das (1990); Madan (1991); Wright (1995); Roy (1996); Stern (1996); Tabor and Gallagher (1995); Friedman 1990; Mumtaz 1991.

[6] Wright (1995).

[7] Juergensmeyer (2000).

[8] Kaplan and Marshall (1996).

[9] Hostetler (1993); Weaver-Zercher (1999).

[10] Gallagher (2008).

[11] Barker (1984).

[12] Gülen (2004).

[13] Gülen (1996).

Unlike sects or cults that tend to isolate their members from societal involvement
while emphasizing strict discipline, authoritarian leadership and rites of membership, the movement has no formal leadership or hierarchy. It has no procedures,
ceremonies or initiation rites for becoming a member. Likewise, the movement has
not been regarded as heretical or extreme by the public, the media or the courts,
either in Turkey or abroad.[14]

While close to a hundred lower court hearings and judgments have been brought
against Mr. Gülen and the movement, based primarily on the contention that he and
his followers are a threat to the secular republic, the major conclusions of the courts
is that the allegations are untrue, baseless and unsubstantiated.[15] Rather, the movement emphasizes respect for the government and participation in the civic life of
Turkey and the countries in which followers reside.

With its participation in education, interfaith and intercultural issues and transnational projects, the Gülen movement is involved in the institutions and activities in
the societies in which its members are located. Its schools around the world follow
the state curriculum and abide by the state's educational criteria. The interfaith and
intercultural events sponsored by the movement attract people from all walks of life
and of all faiths. Rather than isolation from society, Mr. Gülen and his supporters
emphasize involvement and participation in the institutions of society.

Authoritarian Control

Typical of sect or cult movements is authoritarian control by a "charismatic" leader
who is afforded the right to say what the followers will do in all aspects of their
lives, private as well as public. Followers owe the charismatic leader absolute
obedience and respect. The leader is presented as a person with unusual insights
and virtue, one who speaks with authority and merits the right to be unaccountable
to his followers.[16]

While participants in the movement respect Mr. Gülen, study his writings and
sermons, consult him on major issues and projects, and try to live by the principles
he teaches, he has never accepted the description of himself as charismatic leader
of the movement.[17] He regularly admonishes his followers not to refer to the movement
as "the Gülen movement" but rather the "service (hizmet) movement." Likewise,
he rejects the label of "the Gülen schools." Rather, he favors collective consultation
and consensus and argues that it is the millions of participants in the movement that
deserve credit for the successful projects that are outcomes of sharing a worldview

---

[14] Interview with journalist and author Abdullah Aymaz, January, 2005, conducted by Muhammed
Cetin and described in Cetin (2007).
[15] Webb (2000).
[16] Barker (2002).
[17] Akman (1995).

and spirit of commitment. Mr. Gülen initially refused an honorary doctorate from Leeds University in London arguing that it was the millions of dedicated people in the movement who are accomplishing outstanding educational and social service projects. It was only when the honor was awarded in the name of the movement that he ultimately accepted the award.[18]

There is no governing body of the group or administrative hierarchy that issues orders or exercises control over members or activities. Rather, decisions are made by local groups through discussion and consensus. As needs arise in various parts of a country or even internationally, supporters are asked to relocate to assist in a locale where their experience and skills might be needed. For example, teachers are asked to move to an area where new schools are opening. Individuals who have experience in event planning or organization of activities are frequently asked to move to a city where a local group has need of such skills. This frequent relocation of Gülen supporters mitigates against the probability that any one person will emerge as a strong central authority figure.

Visibility/Transparency

Given the millions of people who belong to the movement and who can be found in every sector of society, the movement certainly is not a well-kept secret. In fact, Mr. Gülen's sermons and writings can be accessed on the web, as well as found in hardcopy in bookstores around the world. Therefore, anyone who is interested in Mr. Gülen's ideals and in the movement that he inspires has easy access to his works and to the activities and events sponsored by the hundreds of Gülen-related organizations that exist locally in numerous countries. For example, in Houston, Texas, Gülen supporters founded the Institute of Interfaith Dialog (IID) whose goals are to bring together religious communities in order "to promote compassion, cooperation, partnership and community service through interfaith dialog and conversation. IID is dedicated to encouraging the study of global communities' spiritual traditions from the vantage point of respect, accuracy and appreciation."[19] Similar local organizations exist in many cities throughout the United States. These local groups sponsor such events as interfaith dialog dinners, conferences on issues related to educational and interfaith issues, interfaith and intercultural trips to Turkey, and luncheons with local political and civic leaders. These events are public and serve as a means of engaging the communities in which Gülen followers live, work and study.

Recently the Gülen Institute was established as a joint initiative of the University of Houston in Houston, Texas, and the Institute of Interfaith Dialog. The goal of the Institute is to promote "academic research as well as grass roots activity toward bringing about positive social change, namely, the establishment of stable peace,

---

[18] Interview with Y. Alp Aslandogan, April, 2008.

[19] From the website of the Institute of Interfaith Dialog, Houston, Texas.

social justice, and social harmony by focusing on the themes of education, volunteerism and civic initiatives." The Institute organizes monthly luncheons with a prominent public figure as keynote speaker. Speakers have included James A. Baker and Madeleine Albright, both former U.S. Secretaries of State, the current Chief of Police for the City of Houston and several prominent anchorpersons on local television channels. None of these individuals is associated with the movement. In conversations with several of these high-profile public figures, I learned how thoroughly they had their staffs investigate the Gülen movement before accepting the invitation to speak at the public function. Each of these speakers commended the Gülen Institute for its work toward world peace and dialog. Furthermore, in September, 2008, former U.S. President Bill Clinton delivered a video message at the Ramadan Dinner held in New York City at the Turkish Cultural Center, sponsored by the local Gülen organization. He praised the Gülen movement for the outstanding efforts of its members to promote peace throughout the world.

The involvement of such public political and civic leaders demonstrates two things: (1) the visibility and transparency of the movement; and (2) the fact that the movement has been carefully investigated by these public leaders who cannot afford to align themselves with a group that is "dangerous" or "a threat" to public interests.

Likewise, in my investigations into the finances involved in major projects and companies connected to the movement, I found a high degree of transparency. Not only were top administrators willing to spend time with me and answer the myriad of questions I asked, they also opened their financial records for review. Participants were open and forthcoming in terms of their contributions to the service projects sponsored by the movement.

Modernization (Versus Rejection of Science in Favor of Traditional Values)

The prime example of Mr. Gülen's stance toward modern values of science, technology, rationality, and individual self worth is best demonstrated in the types of schools that he advocated in the 1980s when the first Gülen-inspired schools opened in Turkey. He criticized the *madrasas* (the religious schools in which Islam was taught) and the *tekkes* (unofficial schools established by traditional Sufi orders) because they emphasized spiritual, human and metaphysical values to the exclusion of scientific training and progressiveness. On the other hand, he argued that the secular Turkish schools and military academies impart modern scientific knowledge and technical skills but fail to convey spiritual and ethical values transmitted by Islamic tradition. He saw the root problem as the lack of integration of the new and the old, of modernity and tradition, of scientific and religious knowledge, of technical skills and character formation.[20] Mr. Gülen proposes establishing schools that provide

---

[20] Michels (2005).

quality education in science and technological expertise along with ethical and spiritual values that develop the whole person. His goal is first-rate schools that bring together the latest technological advances with character formation and high ideals.

Mr. Gülen opposes the idea that modernization equals Westernization as some intellectuals in Turkey and throughout the Muslim world assume. He rejects the notion that Islam is a "backward" religion that is an obstacle to progress. Rather, he sees Islam as the "middle way," that is, while it does not reject or condemn the modern scientific approach, neither does it deify it.[21] To engage critically with modernity, Mr. Gülen promotes knowledge and training in the most up to date techniques of science and technology and, at the same time, self transformation in terms of the highest ethical values, love of humankind, positive character traits and the courage to work for the improvement of society. This is summarized in Mr. Gülen's words:

> If intellectuals, educational institutions and mass-media have a vital task to undertake for the good of humanity, it is to deliver modern scientific studies from the lethally polluted atmosphere of materialistic aspirations and ideological fanaticism, and to direct scientists toward true human values.

The Gülen-inspired schools around the world provide quality education in the sciences and modern technology along with the teaching of values, primarily through the example of teachers and principals, many of whom are movement participants and well versed in the ideals promoted by Mr. Gülen.

Nonviolence

Throughout his career as a preacher and teacher, Mr. Gülen has consistently denounced the use of violence as a means toward a political end. In his view, economic conditions, corruption in the state, or ideological reasons can never justify violence. He encourages his listeners and readers to respect the rule of law and to find a peaceful solution to any conflict between individuals, between the individual and the state, or between groups of individuals and the state.[22] A major principle throughout Mr. Gülen's speeches and writings is the avoidance of political and ideological conflict.

Repeatedly Mr. Gülen reiterates the message that he delivered in a full page response in *New York Times* the day after 9/11: "A terrorist cannot be a Muslim, nor can a true Muslim be a terrorist." He says repeatedly that "Islam orders peace and a true Muslim can only be a symbol of peace and the maintenance of basic human rights … The Qur'an, Islam's sacred Book, declares that one who takes a life unjustly is as if he/she took the lives of all humankind, and that one who saves a life is as if he/she saved the lives of all. In the words of our Prophet, a Muslim is one from whom

---

[21] Gülen (1999).

[22] Aslandogan and Cinar (2007).

comes no harm, neither from his/her tongue nor hand."[23] He goes on to reject the philosophy that violence is a legitimate means to a justifiable end. In an address after the London subway bombings and suicide attacks in Israel, he criticized those who condoned such acts: "Unfortunately some condone acts of suicide bombings with the rhetoric of 'they have no other means.' If this is the only means Muslims have, let that means be buried deep in the ground together with the one who uses it."[24]

Mr. Gülen's solution to discontent and human conflicts is change within the individual person. In order to solve social problems such as lack of education, poverty, disadvantage in society and conflict between groups, Mr. Gülen advocates education, mutual respect, providing opportunity to people, and establishing hope for the betterment of the individual and ultimately the society. To achieve these goals, he encourages those who will listen to set up schools that will offer the hope of upward mobility to youth and that will foster interfaith and intercultural dialog and respect. His goal is that these schools will provide an alternative to recruitment into terrorist groups and that the result will be a lasting solution to violent social conflict.

In conclusion, the critics' fear that Turkey's secularism, one of the revered pillars of the Turkish Republic, will be challenged by religiously fanatic groups who favor an Islamic state (i.e. *sharia* law) is understandable given Turkey's history. However, given the data presented in this book, I see no evidence that the Gülen movement has such aims. While it is impossible to say with absolute certainty that the movement will never become a "radical" movement with the aim of overthrowing a legitimate government, the fact that the movement does not display the characteristics usually associated with such sectarian movements makes it highly unlikely that the movement will evolve in such a direction. The fact that the movement is visible and transparent, aims at integration with society rather than isolation from society, is non-authoritarian in structure, does not reject modernization in favor of traditionalism, and condemns violence as a strategy for goal attainment places the movement low on the continuum of qualities that are frequently associated with sectarian or potentially "dangerous" groups in society. Rather, as demonstrated by the fact that Mr. Gülen was invited to give a keynote address at the 2009 World Parliament of Religions in Melbourne, Australia, the Gülen movement is recognized by many in the world as promoting dialog and global peace.

---

[23] Http://en.fGülen.com/content/view/968/2/.

[24] Gülen, "Tolerance, Bombs and Religious Minorities" available online at http://www.herkul.org.

References

Abu-Rabi IM (2008) Editor's introduction. In: Abu-Rabi IM (ed) Contemporary islamic conversations: M. Fethullah Gülen on Turkey, Islam and the West. State University of New York Press, New York

Agai B (2003) The Gülen Movement's Islamic Ethic of Education. In: Yavuz M, Esposito JL (eds) Turkish Islam and the Secular State: The Gülen Movement. The Syracuse University Press.

Agai B (2005) Discursive and Organizational Strategies of the Gülen Movement. Paper presented at: Islam and the Contemporary World: the Fethullah Gülen movement in thought and practice. Rice University, Houston, TX, November

Akman N (1995) Interview with Fethullah Gülen. In Sabah, January 27

Aktay Y (2003) Diaspora and stability. In: Yavuz M, Esposito JL (eds) Turkish Islam and the Secular State: The Gülen Movement. The Syracuse University Press, Syracuse, NY

Akyol M (2008) The context of the Gülen movement: the exceptional story of Turkish Islam. Paper given at the Conference on Islam in the Age of Global Challenges: Alternative Perspectives of the Gülen Movement, Georgetown University

Aras B, Bacik G (2000) The national action party and Turkish politics. Nation Ethnic Politics 6(4):48–64

Aslandogan YA (2006) Defamation as a smoke screen: a case study in modern Turkey. Paper presented at the Second Annual Conference on Islam in the Contemporary World: The Fethullah Gülen Movement in Thought and Practice. The University of Oklahoma in Norman, OK

Aslandogan YA, Cetin M (2006) The educational philosophy of Gülen in thought and practice. In: Hunt RA, AslandoganYA (eds) Muslim citizens of the globalized world: Contributions of the Gülen movement. The Light, Somerset, NJ (Chapter 2)

Aslandogan YA, Cinar B (2007) "A Sunni Muslim scholar's humanitarian and religious rejection of violence against civilians." Paper delivered at the Muslim World in Transition: Contributions of the Gülen Movement Conference, London

Axelrod R (1984) The evolution of cooperation. Basic Books, New York

Aymaz A (2006) Article in Zaman, March 21

Bacik G, Aras B (2002) Exile: a keyword in understanding Turkish politics. Muslim World 92: 387–418

Balci B (2003) Fethullah Gülen's missionary schools in central Asia and their role in the spreading of Turkism and Islam. Religion State Soc 31(2):151–116

Balci T (2007) Turkish Nationalism during the Cold War: The Turkish-Islamic Synthesis. Unpublished dissertation, Claremont Graduate University

Barker E (1984) The making of a Moonie: choice or brainwashing?. Basil Blackwell, New York, NY

Barker E (2002) Introducing new religious movements. Fathom Knowledge Network. Available from: www.fathom.com/feature/121938 (May, 2006, ll.ll)

Baskan F (2004) The political economy of Islamic finance in Turkey: the role of Fethullah Gülen and Asya Finans. In: Henry CM, Wilson R (eds) The politics of Islamic finance. pp 216–239 (Chapter 10) Edinburgh: Edinburgh University Press

Bolukbas E (2008) Interview with the coordinator of information processing. Kimse Yok Mu Solidarity and Aid Association. D. Koc interviewer Istanbul, Turkey April 2007

Bosworth CE, van Donzel E, Heinrichs Wp, Lecomte C (eds) (1997) Encyclopedia of Islam, vol 9. Boston, MA: Brill Publishers

Brewer MB, Kramer RM (1986) Choice behavior in social dilemmas: effects of social identity, group size and decision framing. J Personality Social Psychol 50:543–549

Bromley D, Richardson JT (eds) (1984) The brainwashing/deprogramming controversy. Mellen, Lewiston, NY

Buchanan B (1974) Building organizational commitment: socialization of managers in work organizations. Adm Sci Q 19:533–546

Buechler SM (1999) Social movements in advanced capitalism. Oxford University Press, London

Byrne P (1997) Social movements in Britain. Routledge, London

CAIR (Council on American-Islamic Relations Research Center).(2006). American public opinion about Islam and Muslims. Research Report available at www.cair.com

Cardona P, Lawrence BS, Bentler PM (2004) The influence of social and work exchange relationships on organizational citizenship behavior. Group Organ Manage 29:219–247

Carroll BJ (2007) A dialogue of civilizations: Gülen's Islamic ideals and humanistic discourse. The Light, Somerset, NJ

Cetin M (2005) Mobilization and countermobilization: the Gülen movement in Turkey. Proceedings from Islam in the contemporary world: The Fethullah Gülen movement in thought and practice. Rice University, Houston, TX

Cetin M (2007) The Gülen Movement: its nature and identity. Muslim world in transition: contributions of the Gülen movement. International Conference Proceedings, Leeds Metropolitan University Press, London

Cetin M (2008) Collective identity and action of the Gülen movement: implications for social movement theory. Ph.D. dissertation, Derby University, UK

Cetin M (2009) The Gülen movement: civic service without borders. Blue Dome Press, New York, NY

Collin CS (1960) In: Gibb HAR, Kramers JH, Levi-Provencal E, Schacht J (eds) Encyclopedia of Islam, vol l. Boston, MA: Brill Publishers

Cook SA (2007) Ruling but not governing: the military and political development in Egypt, Algeria and Turkey. Johns Hopkins University Press, Baltimore, MD

Curtis R, Zurcher LA (1974) Social movements: an analytical exploration of organizational forms. Social Problems 21:356–370

Das V (ed) (1990) Mirrors of violence: communities, riots and survivors in South Asia. Oxford University Press, Delhi

Delaney CL (1991) The seed and the soil: gender and cosmology in Turkish village society. University of California, Berkeley

Della Porta D (1995) Social movements, political violence and the state. Cambridge University Press, Cambridge

Della Porta D, Diani M (1999) Social movements: an introduction. Oxford and Blackwell, London

Diyanet Islam Ansiklopedisi (2002) Ankara

Doney PM, Canon JP, Mullen MR (1998) Understanding the influence of national culture on the development of trust. Acad Manage Rev 23:601–620

Ebaugh HR, Koc D (2007) Funding Gülen-inspired good works: demonstrating and generating commitment to the movement. In: Yılmaz İ et al. (eds) International conference proceedings. Muslim World in transition: contributions of the Gülen/Hizmet movement. London conference

Eck D (2001) A new religious America: how a 'Christian Country' has become the most religiously diverse nation on earth. Harper San Francisco, San Francisco

Edwards B, McCarthy JD (2004) Resources and social movement mobilization. In: Snow DA, Soule SA, Kriesi H (eds) The Blackwell companion to social movements. Blackwell, Malden, MA

Ergene ME (2007) Tradition witnessing the modern age: an analysis of the Gülen movement. The Light, New Jersey. Originally published in Turkish as Geleneğin Modern Çağa Tanıklığı: Gülen Hareketinin Analizi (2005)

Ergun ON (1922) Mecelle-I Umur-I Belediye. Istanbul

Eyerman R, Jamison A (1991) Social movements: a cognitive approach. Polity, Cambridge

Fine GA (1986) Friendship in the workplace. In: Derlega VJ, Winstead BA (eds) Friendship and social interaction. Springer, New York

Fireman B, Gamson W (1979) Utilitarian Logic in the Resource mobilization Perspective. In: Zald MN, McCarthy JM (eds) The dynamics of social movements. Winthrop, Cambridge, MA, pp 8–45

Freeman J (1979) Resource mobilization and strategy. In: Zald MN, McCarthy JM (eds) The dynamics of social movements. Winthrop, Cambridge, MA, pp 167–189

Friedman R (1992) Zealots for Zion: inside Israel's West Bank movement. Random House, New York

Fuller G (2008) The New Turkish Republic: Turkey as a pivotal state in the Muslim world. United States Institute of Peace Press, Washington, DC

Gallagher EV (2008) FLDS, Texas O. Religion in the news. Trinity College, Hartford

Gamson WA (1975) The strategy of social protest. Dorsey, Homewood, IL

Garner R (1996) Contemporary movements and ideologies. McGraw-Hill, New York

Gerlach L, Hines V (1970) People, power, change. Bobbs-Merrill, New York

Gülen F (1993) Bahari Soluklarken. Nil Yayinlari, Izmir, p 39

Gülen F (1994) Yitirilmis Cennete Dogru, Towards the Lost Paradise. Izmir, TOV

Gülen F (1998) Toward the lost paradise. Kaynak, Izmir

Gülen F (1999) The relationship of Islam and science and the concept of science. The Fountain Magazine Published by The Light, Inc. Somerset, NJ October–December

Gülen F (2004) In true Islam, terror does not exist. In: Capan E (ed) Terror and suicide attacks: an Islamic perspective. The Light, New Jersey

Gülen F (2005) The state of our souls: revival in Islamic thought and activism. The Light, Somerset, NJ

Gurr T (1970) Why men rebel. Princeton University Press, Princeton, NJ

Hales C (1993) Power, authority and influence. In: Harris A, Bennett N, Preedy M (eds) Organizational effectiveness and improvement in education. Open University Press, Buckingham, Philadelphia

Henry CM, Wilson R (2004) The politics of Islamic finance. Edinburgh University Press, Edinburgh

Hostetler J (1993) Amish society. The John Hopkins University Press, Baltimore, MD

Howard DA (2001) The history of Turkey. Greenwood, Westport, CT

Howe M (2000) Turkey today: a nation divided over Islam's revival. Westview Press, Boulder, Colorado

Hunt RA, Aslandogan YA (eds) (2006) Muslim citizens of the globalized world: contributions of the Gülen movement. The Light, Somerset, NJ

Jacobsen C (1988) Expecting consideration: further insights. Israeli Soc Sci Res 6:83–86

Jenkins JC (1983) Resource mobilization theory and the study of social movements. Ann Rev Sociol 9:527–553

Joireman J, Daniels D, Kamdar D, Duell B (2006) Good citizens to the end? It depends: empathy and concern with future consequences moderate the impact of a short-term horizon on organizational citizenship behaviors. J Appl Psychol 91:1307–1320

Jurgensmeyer M (2000) Terror in the mind of God: the global rise of religious violence. University of California Press, Berkeley, CA

Kalyoncu M (2008) A civilian response to ethno-religious conflict: the Gülen movement in southeast Turkey. Light, NJ

Kanter RM (1968) Commitment and social organization: a study of commitment mechanisms in utopian communities. Am Sociol Rev 33:499–517

Kanter RM (1972) Commitment and community: communes and utopias in sociological perspective. Harvard University Press, Cambridge, MA

Kaplan DE, Marshall A (1996) The cult at the end of the world: the terrifying story of the Aum Doomsday cult. Crown, New York

Karakas v (2002) Nicin Zekat? (Why Zakat?). Timas Yayinlari, Istanbul

Kendall D (2005) Sociology in our times. Thomas Wadsworth, Belmont, CA

Klandermans B (ed) (1989) Organizing for Change: Social movement organizations across cultures. JAI Press, Greenwich, CT

Knoke D (1981) Commitment and detachment in voluntary associations. Am Sociol Rev 46:141–158

Koc D (2008) Generating an understanding of financial resources in the Gülen movement: 'Kimse Yok Mu' Solidarity and Aid Association. Paper presented at the Georgetown Conference, Washington, DC

Komecoglu U (1997) A sociological interpretative approach to the Fethullah Gülen community movement. M.A. thesis (unpublished). Sociology Department, Bogazici University, Istanbul

Konovsky MA, Pugh SD (1994) Citizenship behavior and social exchange. Acad Manage J 37: 656–669

Kraybill DB, Nolt SM (2004) Amish enterprise: from plows to profits. John Hopkins University Press, Baltimore

Kuru AT (2003) Fethullah Gülen's search for a middle way between modernity and Muslim tradition. In: Yavuz MH, Esposito JL (eds) Turkish Islam and the secular state: the Gülen movement. University of Syracuse Press, Syracuse, NY

Kuru AT (2005) Globalization and diversification of Islamist movements: three Turkish cases. Pol Sci Q 120(2):253–274

Madan TN (1991) The double-edged sword: fundamentalism and the Sikh religious tradition. In: Marty ME, Appleby RS (eds) Fundamentalisms observed. University of Chicago Press, Chicago

Magnarella PJ (1974) Tradition and change in a Turkish town. Halsted, New York

Mardin S (1989) Religion and social change in modern Turkey: the case of Bediuzzaman Said Nursi. The State University of New York Press, Albany, NY

Mason W (2000) The future of political Islam in Turkey. World Pol J XVII(2):56–67

McAdam D, McCarthy JD, Zald MN (1988) Social movements. In: Smelser NJ (ed) The handbook of sociology. Sage, Beverly Hills, CA, pp 695–737

McAdam D, McCarthy JD, Zald MN (1996) Introduction: opportunities, mobilizing structures and framing processes – Toward a synthetic, comparative perspective on social movements. In: McAdam D, McCarthy JD, Zald MN (eds) Comparative perspectives on social movements: political opportunities, mobilizing structures and cultural framings. Cambridge University Press, Cambridge

McCarthy JD, Wolfson M (1996) Resource mobilization by local social movement organizations: agency, strategy and organization in the movement against drinking and driving. Am Sociol Rev 61:1070–1088

McCarthy JD, Zald MN (1977) Resource mobilization and social movements: a partial theory. Am J Sociol 82:1212–1241

McChesney RD (1995) Charity and philanthropy in Islam: institutionalizing the call to do good. Indiana University Press, Indianapolis

Mecham RQ (2004) From the ashes of virtue, a promise of light: the transformation of political Islam in Turkey. Third World Q 25(2):339–358

Melucci A (1999) Challenging codes: collective action in the information age. Cambridge University Press, Cambridge, UK

Michel T (2003) Fethullah Gülen as Educator. In: Yavuz MH, Esposito JL (eds) Turkish Islam and the Secular State: the Gülen movement. Syracuse University Press, Syracuse, NY (Chapter 4)

Michels T (2005) Sufism and modernity in the thought of Fethullah Gülen. Muslim World 95(3):341–358

Michels T (2008) Welcoming address, presented at: Islam in the Age of Global Challenges Conference. Georgetown University, Washington, DC, November

Morris AD, Staggenborg S (2004) Leadership in social movements. In: Snow DA, Soule SA, Kriesi H (eds) The Blackwell companion to social movements. Blackwell, Malden, MA

Mumtaz A (1991) Islamic Fundamentalism in South Asia: Jamaat-i-Islami and Tablighi Jamaat of South Asia. In: Martin M, Appleby RS (eds) Fundamentalisms observed. University of Chicago Press, Chicago (Chapter 8)

Nugent PD, Abolafia MY (2006) The creation of trust through interaction and exchange: the role of consideration in organizations. Group Organ Manage 31:628–650

Oberschall A (1973) Social conflict and social movements. Prentice Hall, Englewood Cliffs, NJ

Oliver P, Marwell G (1992) Mobilizing technologies for collective action. In: Morris A, Mueller C (eds) Frontiers of social movement theory. Yale University Press, New Haven, CT, pp 251–172

Olson EA (1965) The logic of collective action. Cambridge University Press, Cambridge, MA

Ozdalga E (2000) Worldly asceticism in Islamic casting: Fethullah Gülen's inspired piety and activism. Critique: Crit Middle Eastern Stud 17:84–104

Park W (2007) The Fethullah Gülen movement as a transnational phenomenon. In: Yılmaz İ et al. (eds) International conference proceedings. Muslim world intTransition: contributions of the Gülen movement. Leeds Metropolitan Press, London

Piece JE (1964) Life in a Turkish village. Holt, Rinehart and Winston, New York

Pope H (2005) Sons of the conquerors: the rise of the Turkish world. Overlook Press, New York, NY

Read JG (2004) Culture, class and work among Arab-American women. LFB Scholarly Publishing, New York

Read JG, Bartowski JP (2000) To veil or not to veil: a case study of identity negotiation among Muslim women in Austin, Texas. Gender Soc 14(3):395–417

Reader I (1996) A poisonous cocktail: Aum Shrinrikyo's path to violence. Nordic Institute of Asian Studies, Copenhagen

Rioux SM, Penner LA (2001) The causes of organizational citizenship behavior: a motivational analysis". J Appl Psychol 86:1306–1314

Robbins T, Anthony D (eds) (1990) In Gods we trust. Transaction, New Brunswick, NJ

Roy JT (ed) (1996). False patriots: the threat of antigovernment extremists. Southern Poverty Law Center, Klanwatch Project, Montgomery, Alabama

Sakin M, Albayrak M (2007) *Zaman* newspaper, p 5

Salamon LM, Sokolowski W, List R (2003) The Johns Hopkins comparative nonprofit sector project. Johns Hopkins Center for Civil Society Studies, Baltimore, p 70

Saritoprak Z (2005) An Islamic approach to peace and nonviolence: a Turkish experience. Muslim World 95(3):413–428

Saritoprak Z, Griffith S (2005) Fethullah Gülen and the 'People of the Book': a voice from Turkey for interfaith dialogue". Muslim World 95(3):329–340

Sevendi N (1997) The New York interview with Fethullah Gülen. Sabah Kitaplari, Istanbul

Sevendi N (2008) Contemporary Islamic conversations: M. Fethullah Gülen on Turkey, Islam and the West. State University of New York Press, New York

Singer A (2002) Constructing Ottoman beneficence: an imperial soup kitchen in Jerusalem. SUNY, New York

Smelser NJ (1962) Theory of collective behavior. Free Press, New York

Snow DA, Zurcher LA, Ekland-Olson S (1980) Social networks and social movements: a micro-structural approach to differential recruitment. Am Sociol Rev 45:787–801

Solberg A (2005) The Gülen schools: a perfect compromise or comprising perfectly? Paper read at the Kotor Network Conference

Sprinzak E (1991) The process of delegitimization: towards a linkage theory of political terrorism. In: McCauley C (ed) Terrorism and public policy. Frank Cass, London

Stern KS (1996) A force upon the plain: the American militia movement and the politics of hate. New York University Press, New York

Tabor JD, Gallagher EV (1995) Why Waco: cults and the battle for religious freedom in America. University of California Press, Berkeley, CA

Tapper R (1991) Introduction. In Tapper R (ed). Islam in Modern Turkey: Religion, politics and literature in a secular state. I.B. Tauris, London

Tekalan SA (2005) A movement of volunteers. Proceedings from Islam in the contemporary world: the Fethullah Gülen movement in thought and practice. Rice University, Houston, TX

The Book of Dede Korkut (1974) Translation, introduction and notes by Geoffrey Lewis. Penguin, New York

Tilly C (1978) From mobilization to revolution. Addison-Wesley, Reading, MA

Tolson J (2008) Finding the voices of moderate Islam. Faith Matters (www.usnews.com)

Turam B (2004) A bargain between the secular state and Turkish Islam: politics of ethnicity in Central Asia. Nations Nationalism 10:353–374

Turner R, Killian L (1972) Collective behavior, 2nd edn. Prentice Hall, Englewood Cliffs, NJ

Unal A (2007) The Qur'an with annotated interpretation in modern English. The Light Publ, Somerset, NJ

Unal A, Williams A (2000) Fethullah Gülen: advocate of dialogue. The Fountain, Fairfax, VA

Van VM, DeCremer D (1999) Leadership in social dilemmas: the effects of group identification on collective actions to provide public goods. J Pers Soc Psychol 67:126–141

Weaver-Zercher D (1999) Putting the Amish the work: Mennonites and the Amish culture market, 1950–1975. Church Hist March 68:1

Webb LE (2000) Fethullah Gülen: is there more to him than meets the eye?. Mercury, Izmir

Weller P (2006) Fethullah Gülen, religions, globalization and dialogue. In: Hunt RA, Aslandogan YA (eds) Muslim citizens of the globalized world: Contributions of the Gülen movement. The Light, Somerset, NJ

Woodhall R (2005) Organizing the organization, educating the educators: an examination of Fethullah Gülen's teaching and the membership of the movement. Proceedings from Islam in the contemporary world: the Fethullah Gülen movement in thought and practice. Rice University, Houston, TX

Wright SA (ed) (1995) Armageddon in Waco: Critical perspectives on the Branch Davidian conflict. University of Chicago Press, Chicago

Wuthnow R (2005) America and the challenges of religious diversity. Princeton University Press, NJ

Yavuz MH (1999) Search for a new social contract in Turkey: Fethullah Gülen, the virtue party and the kurds. SAIS Rev 19(1):114–143

Yavuz MH (2002) The Gülen movement: The Turkish Puritans. In: Yavuz MH, Esposito JL (eds) Turkish Islam and the secular state: the Gülen movement. Syracuse University Press, Syracuse, NY (Chapter 2)

Yavuz MH (2003a) Islam in the Public Sphere: the Case of the Nur Movement. In: Yavuz MH, Esposito JL (eds) Turkish Islam and the Secular State: the Gülen movement. Syracuse University Press, Syracuse, NY (Chapter l)

Yavuz MH (2003b) The Gülen Movement: The Turkish Puritans. In: Yavuz MH, Esposito JL (eds) Turkish Islam and the Secular State: the Gülen movement. Syracuse University Press, Syracuse, NY (Chapter 2)

Yavuz MH (2005) Cleansing Islam from the public sphere. Posted on the website for the Sunni Razvi Society International, General Islamic Topics, on March 2, 2005

Yavuz MH, Esposito JL (2003) Introduction. In: Yavuz MH, Esposito JL (eds) Turkish Islam and the secular state: the Gülen movement. Syracuse University Press, Syracuse, NY

Yediyıldız B (2003) XVIII. Yüzyılda Türkiyede Vakıf Müessesi, Bir Sosyal tarih İncelemesi [A Socio-historical analysis of waqf institutions in 18th century Turkey]. Türk Tarih Kurumu, Ankara

Yilmaz I (2003) Ijtihad and Tacdid by conduct. In: Yavuz MH, Esposito JL (eds) Turkish Islam and the secular state: the Gülen movement. Syracuse University Press, Syracuse, NY

Yilmaz I (2005) State, Law, Civil Society and Islam in Contemporary Turkey. The Muslim World, vol 95, No. 3. Special Issue: Islam in Contemporary Turkey: the Contributions of Gülen: 385–412

Yousef TM (2004) The *Murabaha* Syndrome in Islamic finance: laws, institutions and politics. In: Henry CM, Wilson R (eds) The politics of Islamic finance. Edinburgh University Press, Edinburgh, England, pp 63–80 (Chapter 3)

Zald MN, Ash R (1966) Social movements organizations: growth, decay and change". Soc Forces 44:327–340

Zald MN, McCarthy JD (eds) (1979) The dynamics of social movements: resource mobilization, social control and tactics. Winthrop, Cambridge, MA

Zeskind L (1986) The "Christian Identity" Movement: analyzing its theological rationalization for racist and anti-Semitic violence. Division of Church and Society of the National Council of the Churches of Christ in the U.S.A., New York

Tuncer F Foundations of the intellectual development of Fethullah Gülen. Translated by Aslandogan YA